FREE TO FORGIVE

Robert Jeffress

With Learning Activities and Leader Guide by
Susan A. Lanford

EVERYDAY DISCIPLESHIP SERIES

LifeWay Press
Nashville, Tennessee

ISBN 0-6330-0900-8

Dewey Decimal Classification: 177
Subject Heading: FORGIVENESS

This book is the text for course CG-0580
in the subject area Personal Life
of the Christian Growth Study Plan

Unless otherwise indicated, Scripture quotations are from the Holy Bible, *New International Version*, copyright 1973, 1978, 1984 by International Bible Society

Printed in the United States of America

As God works through us, we will help people and churches know Jesus Christ and seek His kingdom by providing biblical solutions that spiritually transform individuals and churches.

LifeWay Press
127 Ninth Avenue, North
Nashville, TN 37234

Meet the Authors

Dr. Robert Jeffress

Dr. Robert Jeffress is pastor of the 8500-member First Baptist Church in Wichita Falls, Texas. His television program "Pathway to Victory" is seen weekly on the FamilyNet and the Inspiration networks. Dr. Jeffress is the author of eight books including *As Time Runs Out* (Broadman & Holman) and *When Forgiveness Doesn't Make Sense* (Waterbrook Press).

Susan A. Lanford

Susan A. Lanford has been a freelance writer and consultant for family issues for almost 15 years. Most recently she has worked in the areas of stress management and chronic symptom management with a behavioral medicine approach in corporate and hospital-based settings. Her educational background has focused on pastoral care and family systems study with degrees from Texas Christian University and Southwestern Baptist Theological Seminary as well as additional study in marriage and family therapy at Texas Woman's University.

Contents

INTRODUCTION
The View from the Pulpit

"Forgiveness," C.S. Lewis once observed, "is a beautiful word, until you have something to forgive." The issue of forgiveness touches us every day. Sometimes we experience a major crisis that forces us to choose whether or not to forgive or to be forgiven. More often, our issues of forgiveness involve lesser offenses. In my experiences as a pastor, I have discovered that regardless of the size of the offense, we do not usually choose forgiveness as the preferred response. Why do we Christians, who have been forgiven so much, have such difficulty forgiving others? I believe at least three factors add to our difficulty:

1. First, it is hard to impart to another person what you have not experienced. We learn how to forgive from our Father in heaven, for only the forgiven can truly forgive. But if experiencing God's grace is the only requirement for forgiving, then it stands to reason that the church would be filled with forgiving people. Sadly, however, some of the most unforgiving people you ever encounter are those in pews on Sunday mornings. My former pastor, W.A. Criswell, once said, "If I ever fall into a sin, I pray that I don't fall into the hands of those censorious, critical, self-righteous judges in the church." What an indictment! Yet, we know it is the truth. Why?

2. Many people, including Christians, find it difficult to forgive for a second reason. We really don't understand what real forgiveness is, and isn't. I frequently counsel with people who would genuinely like to let go of years of bitterness, but will not do so because they are waiting for their offender's repentance or rehabilitation. They have been taught that it is impossible to forgive someone who first does not ask for forgiveness.

3. A third reason many people struggle to forgive is the danger of the unbalanced seesaw. Remember what it was like to play on a seesaw? As long as your playmate was approximately the same weight as you, everything worked fine. But what happened when a mischievous friend jumped off the seesaw while you were still on it? Crash! Now imagine a seesaw with one side labeled "guilt" and the other "blame." The only way to keep this seesaw in balance is to have enough "blame" to balance the "guilt." The more guilt you feel for your own mistakes, the more blame needed to remain in emotional equilibrium. What happens if you suddenly get rid of the blame toward others without also removing your guilt? You will emotionally "crash." We hesitate to forgive people because it is much easier, and safer, to blame others for our problems than to blame the seemingly logical culprit. At some point in every life, people cry out, "Why did God allow this hurt in my life?"

I pray that you will find in this study and in your group discussions both the encouragement and practical instruction you need to let go of any hurt and experience that soul-quenching relief that comes with forgiveness. I hope the biblical truths in this study will help you to give wise counsel to those who are struggling with issues of guilt forgiveness.

Study Plan

Unlike many other LifeWay discipleship resources, the units of this study are not divided into daily increments. Still, we encourage you to study two to three pages per day in preparation for your weekly meeting. Before your small group meets, go over your unit of study and review what you have learned. May God bless you as you study the important topic of forgiveness.

PART ONE

When Forgiveness Doesn't Make Sense

Dawn Smith Jordan learned about forgiveness the hard way. A few years ago during a church service, she shared with us her dramatic story (also the basis for a television movie, Nightmare in Columbia County).

On May 31, 1985, Dawn's 17-year-old sister, Shari Smith, was abducted while walking from her car to the mailbox. Five days later Shari's body was discovered. Soon afterward the Smith family received a letter written by Shari. The kidnapper allowed her to write it before he murdered her. Then he mailed her letter.

Shari called her letter "my last will and testament." She wrote: "I love you all so much. Please don't let this ruin your lives. Keep living one day at a time for Jesus. Don't worry about me because I know I'm going to be with my Father." The letter concluded, "All my love, Shari."

Unfortunately, the family's nightmare was far from over. The killer telephoned them numerous times, cruelly describing the gruesome details of Shari's murder. Ultimately, he was apprehended and received two death sentences for his brutal crime. In her testimony Dawn revealed how she remembered thinking: *Now the story is finally finished. I can attempt to rebuild my shattered life.*

A few years later, however, she received a letter that would forever change her life. The killer wrote to Dawn that he had become a Christian. "Dawn," he asked, "will you and your family ever forgive me for what I have done?"

Stop for a moment—ask yourself how you would respond to that question if you were in the Smith family's situation. Dawn shared with us: "As a Christian, I knew that when somebody wrongs you, you forgive them. That's basic knowledge. Yet, suddenly, forgiveness was a lot harder to do." In her honest struggle, God led Dawn to Ephesians 4:32: "Be kind and compassionate to one another, forgiving each other, just as in Christ God forgave you."

"It wasn't easy," Dawn said. "It wasn't overnight. But God gave me the answer that I needed. We are to forgive just as Jesus forgave us. I was finally able to sit down and write a letter to Shari's killer, telling him that only because of the grace that I have received in my own life could I let him know that he was forgiven."[1]

Unit One

Being Forgiven, But Not a Forgiver

An inseparable link binds the receiving of God's forgiveness and the granting of forgiveness to others. The truth of the verse, "Just as in Christ God forgave you," is the bridge that relates grace to forgiveness. Can only Christians forgive? Of course not. Non-Christians choose to let go of offenses as trivial as being cut off in traffic or as major as marital infidelity. But the Bible teaches that Christians should find it easier to forgive as a result of the grace they have experienced in their own lives.

Remember the story of Jesus in the home of Simon the Pharisee? A woman (most likely a prostitute) crashed Simon's dinner party and approached Jesus with a vial of expensive perfume. "As she stood behind him at his feet weeping, she began to wet his feet with her tears. Then she wiped them with her hair, kissed them and poured perfume on them" (Luke 7:38). The woman's actions caused quite a stir among the invited guests. Simon, who prided himself with keeping the law, was thoroughly disgusted by the woman's presence in his home, not to mention her treatment of Jesus. Simon thought to himself, *If this Jesus is truly a prophet, then he would know this woman is a prostitute* (see v. 39).

Jesus had a little fun with his host and, at the same time, left no doubt regarding His own identity. "Simon," He announced, "I have something to say to you!" Then Jesus related the following vignette to Simon and his dinner guests:

"Two men owed money to a certain moneylender. One owed him five hundred denarii, and the other fifty. Neither of them had the money to pay him back, so he canceled the debts of both. Now which of them will love him more?" (Luke 7:41-42).

Perceptive enough to realize where this conversation was going, Simon answered: "I suppose the one he forgave more." Bingo! Simon got it right, for Jesus responded, "You have judged correctly." Jesus continued: "Do you see this woman? I entered your house; you gave Me no water for My feet, but she has wet My feet with her tears, and wiped them with her hair. You gave Me no kiss; but she, since the time I came in, has not ceased to kiss My feet. You did not anoint My head with oil, but she anointed My feet with perfume. For this reason I say to you, her sins, which are many, have been forgiven, for she loved much; but he who is forgiven little, loves little" (7:44-47).

Frankly, it's quite easy to make the wrong application from this story. In fact, I'm certain that Simon, infected with a serious case of self-righteousness, completely missed Jesus' point. I can imagine Simon concluded: "I understand what You're saying, Jesus. Big sinners have a lot more to be thankful for than little sinners like me. If I were a filthy prostitute like her, I probably would throw myself at your feet, too. Thank God I'm not in that condition!"

Simon understood that only sinners need forgiveness. Earlier Jesus made that point to a group of Pharisees (perhaps including Simon) who objected to His dining with tax gatherers and sinners: "It is not the healthy who need a doctor, but the sick. I have not come to call the righteous, but sinners to repentance" (Luke 5:31-32). What Simon failed to understand, as do so many others today, was that he was among those who were spiritually sick and in need of forgiveness.

We all need forgiveness for both small and large offenses. Recall some of those offenses in your life and record them below:

Small Offenses Needing Forgiveness	Large Offenses Needing Forgiveness
_____	_____
_____	_____
_____	_____

Who, if anyone, offered you forgiveness? Write their names to the left of the offense. Of whom, if anyone, did you ask forgiveness? Write their names to the right of the offense.

A number of years ago my mom was diagnosed with colon cancer and told that she had only four months to live. During the final days of her life, a local television station interviewed her about her illness and her courage in facing death. "Mrs. Jeffress," the interviewer asked, "how does it feel to know that you are terminal?"

"The truth is," my mom quickly answered with her unique combination of wit and wisdom, "we are all terminal. The only difference is that some of us realize it and some of us don't."

That truth was the only real difference between the prostitute and Simon. Both suffered from the terminal disease of sin. Both were in danger of eternal death. Both were in need of supernatural healing from Jesus—but only the repentant woman understood her need for forgiveness; Simon denied his.

This is a good time to reflect on your own attitude about sin in your life and to consider how often you apply words such as *guilt, repent,* and *Father, forgive me* to yourself and your life.

On separate paper, write a letter to Jesus. Explain your need for forgiveness. When you've finished, pray over your letter. You may want to record your thoughts and feelings after you've prayed. Keep this letter at this place in your book.

Forgiven People Can Forgive

Forgiven people are in a better position to extend grace than those who are unforgiven because they have three distinct advantages:

1. Forgiven People Understand Their Own Guilt

Christians should be better forgivers than non-Christians because they've been forced to admit their own failures. Simon the Pharisee imagined a wide gap between himself and the prostitute, so he felt contempt for her. After all, he was a religious leader and she was a woman of the night. Jesus devoted much of His teaching against this supposed morality gulf between the religious leaders and ordinary people. When we realize that the moral gulf between us and our offender is not significant in God's eyes, we remove a tremendous barrier to forgiveness.

Think of one person you feel has wronged you more than anyone else. On the thermometer in the margin, mark the degree of separation the wrong created in your relationship.

Think of the sin in your life that required Jesus' death to provide forgiveness. On the thermometer mark the spot indicating the degree of separation your sin created with God.

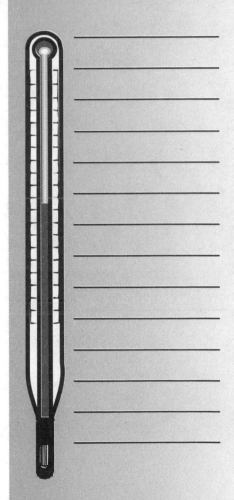

Reflect on the two drawings. What do you observe that helps you to understand your own guilt? being wronged? being forgiven? Note your reflections in the margin.

In God's eyes, we all need forgiveness. All are guilty before Him. In God's economy, no difference separates the preacher and the prostitute, the governor and the gunman, or the sophisticate and the savage. The Book of Romans reveals how we can receive God's forgiveness. The first three chapters explain our guilt before God.

In your Bible, read Romans 3:9-12. Underline every phrase that describes how many of us are sinners.

Did you catch them all? "None righteous ... not one ... no one understands ... no one seeks God ... no one does good." Just in case anyone missed Paul's point, he added the familiar words: "For all have sinned and fall short of the glory of God" (Rom. 3:23).

Every year in Vacation Bible School, I illustrate this truth to our children by acting out a silly scenario with our ministers of education and music. I ask the children to imagine the three of us standing on a California beach. In a moment of insanity, we decide to swim to Hawaii. We all jump in the water at the same time. After the first mile, our minister of music gives up and sinks to the bottom; after five miles our minister of education succumbs to exhaustion; but the pastor, being in great physical shape (the kids erupt in laughter at this remark), swims one hundred miles before giving up.

Then I ask the question, "Who made it to Hawaii?" Even though two of us swam farther than the music minister, and I outdistanced the minister of education, we all became food for the fish.

Think who you would most like to understand the truth, "For all have sinned and fall short of the glory of God," regardless of age or circumstance? What illustration can you conceive to best explain this truth to him or her? Record your illustration here.

_____

_____

If it is possible, share the illustration with this person before meeting again with your group. Use the space in the margin to describe your conversation.

Compared to the holiness of God, differences in goodness between human beings are negligible. Regardless of our individual virtues, we all fall woefully short of the perfection God demands. Realizing this truth is not only the foundation for receiving God's forgiveness, but also it is the basis for extending forgiveness to others.

In *The Gulag Archipelago,* the great Russian writer Aleksandr Solzhenitsyn tells of befriending an army officer in World War II. Their shared convictions and dreams formed what seemed to be an unbreakable bond. But after the war, they went in opposite directions. Solzhenitsyn was thrown into a Russian gulag for his unrelenting courage. His friend became an interrogator who brutally tortured prisoners to gain confessions. How can these differences between two men who had been so similar be explained? Solzhenitsyn refused to believe that he was totally good and his friend was totally evil. Instead, Solzhenitsyn wrote:

> If only it were all so simple! If only there were evil people ... committing evil deeds, and it were necessary only to separate them from the rest of us and destroy them. But the line dividing good and evil cuts through the heart of every human being. And who is willing to destroy a piece of his own heart?
>
> One and the same human being is, at various ages, under various circumstances, a totally different human being. At times he is close to being a devil, at times to sainthood.[2]

When we understand that the same evil that motivated our offender to hurt us resides in our heart as well, we're in a much better position to forgive.

Record the first advantage Christians have in forgiving:

_____

_____

Reflecting on what you've learned from this section, complete this statement: I understand my guilt well enough to know ...

_____

_____

2. Forgiven People Understand the Need for Intervention

One of the greatest barriers to forgiveness is believing that our offender must demonstrate some remorse and desire for reconciliation before we can honestly forgive that person. The truth is that sometimes the offended party must take the first step to restore a fractured relationship.

Several days ago I punished one of my daughters for disobedience. After pronouncing the sentence of no television for several days, she stormed to her room, yelling about the unfairness of it all and expressing her strong desire for a new father. Believe me, remorse and repentance were nowhere in sight. Since I was the one who was wronged, I clearly would have been within my rights to allow her to suffer the consequences of her outburst. I could have decided not to talk with her until she realized she was wrong. I'm emotionally stronger than she and I could wait her out, but my love for her and desire for reconciliation overshadowed my sense of justice.

I went looking for her and knocked on her bedroom door. No answer. Quietly turning the doorknob, I entered and heard her sobbing uncontrollably—but I couldn't see her anywhere. She had crawled under the bed. So I crawled under the bed, too. After calmly reviewing her transgressions and why punishment was warranted, I reached over and pulled her close to me. I reassured her of my love and willingly forgave her. In an instant our relationship was restored.

Those who demand repentance from their offenders before granting forgiveness often point to Ephesians 4:32 or Colossians 3:13 to defend the position. They say: "The Bible tells us to forgive one another the same way God forgave us. If God demands that we repent of our sins, why shouldn't we insist that our offender demonstrate that same kind of remorse before we forgive him?"

Record your answer to the above question.

_____

_____

It's a good question and one that we'll deal with more specifically in unit two. But we must remember that God is the One who always takes the initiative in forgiving. Although He is the offended party, He is also the One who first seeks reconciliation with us.

The Bible's first recorded act of forgiveness illustrates this wonderful truth. Genesis 3 reveals how sin first entered the world. The serpent, empowered by Satan, seduced the man and woman into eating from the one tree God declared off-limits. God would have been completely justified in killing them immediately. Instead, as recorded in the remainder of Genesis 3, God initiated reconciliation:

> Then the man and his wife heard the sound of the Lord God as he was walking in the garden in the cool of the day, and they hid from the Lord God among the trees of the garden. But the Lord God called to the man, "Where are you?" (3:8-9).

Although Adam and Eve had lost their way, God went searching for them. After explaining the consequences of their actions, He then covered their actions by providing them clothing. "The Lord God made garments of skin for Adam and his wife and clothed them" (v. 21).

Adam and Eve were wearing fig-leaf garments they had constructed immediately following their sin. By this action, they had demonstrated their sense of guilt and their need for a covering.

Guilt is indeed one consequence of sin, though I hesitate to use the word because it's too often used as a synonym for an illegitimate emotion to be rooted out of our lives at any cost. Some guilt certainly is illegitimate. But the main reason most people feel guilty is because they are guilty. Adam and Eve did not need a preacher to tell them they were guilty. Their transgression motivated them to cover themselves with a pitiful collection of fig leaves—an outward admission of that guilt.

Adam and Eve needed to recognize another truth before they could clothe themselves with custom-made garments from God: they had to acknowledge the inadequacy of their self-made covering. Though the fig-leaf clothing hid the couple's nakedness, it did not hide nor remove their shame. This could happen only with the more effective covering God would provide. In the same way, you and I must first admit our own inadequacies before we can receive God's forgiveness.

James Montgomery Boice compares our good works to Monopoly money. As long as you're only playing Monopoly, those blue 50s and yellow 100s are of tremendous value. But they're absolutely worthless in the real world. (If you don't believe me, just try sending them for your next mortgage payment!) In the same way, our good deeds are like "filthy rags" in the sight of God (Isa. 64:6). In God's economy, they're as worthless as play money.

Psychologist Rollo May once observed that man is the only animal that runs faster when he has lost his way.

Although our good works might be useful in hiding the true condition of our souls from others, they're useless in the sight of God.

13

Which of your good deeds do you want God to notice?

_____

What do you hope He'll observe in that good deed?

_____

What motivates you to do good deeds?

_____

Receiving God's forgiveness requires a realization of our need and of our inadequacy. But note that God required nothing of Adam and Eve before He initiated the reconciliation process. He came looking for them. He prepared the covering before they ever acknowledged their need for a covering. And God does the same for each of us.

Consider these passages that speak of God's initiative in meeting our need for forgiveness. Look up each passage listed below and write the truths you discover in your own words:

Romans 5:6 _____

Ephesians 2:4-5_____

1 John 4:10 _____

While repentance and remorse are necessary to receive forgiveness, they are not required for granting forgiveness.

Although repentance is a necessary ingredient to experience God's forgiveness, we must never forget that God made all the first moves to bring reconciliation with His creatures. That's why Christians, more than all others, should understand that sometimes the offended party must take the first step to restore a broken relationship.

In the margin record the second advantage Christians have in offering forgiveness.

How will your life be different if you truly accept that you have this advantage?

_____

_____

3. Forgiven People Understand Grace

Several decades ago at a British conference on comparative religions, a group of experts were discussing the uniqueness of Christianity—what differentiates Christianity from other religions. When C. S. Lewis entered the room, he remarked, "Oh, that's easy. It's grace."

After additional discussion, the participants agreed. The idea of God's love being free of charge and having no strings attached is a novel idea. Every other religion emphasizes man's responsibility to secure God's approval. Only Christianity makes God's love unconditional.[3]

What is grace? Compose a definition and write it below.

_____

With that definition in mind, recall an instance when you were the recipient of such grace from another person. Describe that instance and how it made you feel.

_____

_____

Think of a time when you extended such grace to another person. Describe that instance and how it made you feel.

_____

_____

Here's my definition: Grace is a deliberate decision to give something good to someone who doesn't deserve it. A woman shared with me that

Grace is a deliberate decision to give something good to someone who doesn't deserve it.

her husband had been engaged in a year-long affair. Though she had biblical grounds to divorce him, she chose to rebuild her marriage. She gave her undeserving husband a second chance. She gave him grace.

The basis for all grace is God's offer to release us from the consequences of our sin. We deserve eternal punishment, but He offers to release us from that punishment and to give us eternal life instead.

God's action is not without cost. Grace does not mean that He simply overlooks our sin, as I might choose to ignore my child's disrespectful tone or disobedient act. God's holy nature will not allow Him to simply ignore our sin. "I will not acquit the guilty," God said in Exodus 23:7. "The Lord will not leave the guilty unpunished" (Nah. 1:3).

So how can a righteous God extend grace without violating His own nature? If God does not demand that I pay for my sin, then someone else must pay. If God does not hold me responsible for my transgressions, He must hold someone else responsible.

That person is Jesus Christ; the Savior was held responsible for our sins. The apostle Paul explained: "God made him who had no sin to be sin for us, so that in him we might become the righteousness of God" (2 Cor. 5:21). These words describe the most amazing transaction in history, and they refer to two exchanges that took place when Jesus was on the cross. First, Jesus Christ assumed the obligation for our sin. He "knew no sin," but God made Him "to be sin on our behalf." This does not mean that Jesus became a sinner, but that He paid the obligation for our sins.

Philip Yancey recounts a scene from the movie *The Last Emperor.* The brother of the young emperor of China asked, "What happens when you do wrong?" The boy emperor replied, "When I do wrong, someone else is punished." To demonstrate his words, he broke a jar, then had one of his many servants beaten.[4] God has reversed that pattern. As His servants, we all have erred, but God, in the person of Jesus Christ, received the punishment each of us deserved.

List as many words or phrases as you can think of that describe the act of assuming blame that is not yours. For example, you might say: "I've been framed."

_____

_____

Perhaps your list includes words like: unjustly accused; "You've got the wrong guy!"; witch hunt; scapegoat; fall guy; whipping boy.

〜〜〜

Describe the feelings such words stir in you.

_____

Consider the second part of the transaction that God performed—"that we might become the righteousness of God." When I become a Christian, not only does God place my sin on Christ, but also He takes the righteousness of Christ, credits it to my spiritual bank account, and "justifies" me (meaning, "to declare not guilty").

Paul wrote in Romans 4:5: "to the man who does not work but trusts God who justifies the wicked, his faith is credited as righteousness." This word *credited* is an accounting term meaning, "to place to someone's account." When I trust in Christ as my Savior, God not only credits Christ with my sin, but also He credits me with all the righteousness of Christ. Perhaps this illustration will clarify.

Suppose you want to purchase a home, but your financial statement is a mess. That's the bad news. The good news is Bill Gates is your father. Dear old Dad, seeing your dilemma, tells you: "I want to help. I will assume the responsibility for your debt. When you see the bank officer tomorrow, instead of submitting your financial statement, use mine."

How would you respond to such an offer? If you were filled with pride (and incredible stupidity), you might say: "Forget it, Dad. I don't need your help." Or, you could say: "Dad, I need your help. I've made some bad decisions. I'm practically bankrupt. So I'll accept your generous offer." When you submit your loan request with your father's financial statement, your application is based on his resources, not yours. His riches are more than sufficient to cover your mortgage.

The story illustrates the most profound truth in the universe. God's law demands that if you're going to secure a home in heaven, you must be perfect. Your goodness must equal that of Jesus Christ. The problem is we're all morally and spiritually bankrupt. You may have more righteousness in your spiritual bank account than I do, and I may possess more than Adolf Hitler, but it doesn't matter. None of us has enough.

Yet God has extended to us a gracious offer: "If you would like, I will consider your application for heaven based on My Son's spiritual resources rather than your own, and His righteousness is more than enough to make up for your deficiency."

Amazingly, most people reject God's offer. But those who accept God's invitation are in the best position to understand what grace is all about—granting to others what they do not deserve, earn, or sometimes even request.

On December 1, 1997, a dozen students gathered to pray before the beginning of classes at Heath High School in Paducah, Kentucky. As they concluded their prayer time, a 14-year-old freshman carrying a gun approached the group and began shooting. Three students died and five others were seriously wounded. For weeks, parents, school officials, and the media were at a loss to explain such a vile act.

Many people were equally astounded by the willingness of survivors and family members of the deceased to forgive the shooter and his family. One such person was 15-year-old Melissa Jenkins, who expects to spend the rest of her life as a paraplegic as a result of spinal cord damage from the shooting. Yet Melissa, a Christian, sent this message through a friend to the one who devastated her life: "Tell him I forgive him."[5]

Obviously not all Christians react like Melissa Jenkins. Though they may have come to terms with their own sin, pled for God's intervention, and experienced the grace transaction firsthand, they still refuse to extend that same grace to others. What are the consequences of this "ungrace"? The answers are the focus of unit two.

Record the third advantage Christians have in forgiving:

_____

Use the space in the margin to complete this statement: I understand God's grace well enough to know ...

---

[1] Transcript of testimony by Dawn Smith Jordan given at First Baptist Church, Wichita Falls, Texas, on 10 September 1995.

[2] A. I. Solzhenitsyn, *The Gulag Archipelago* (New York: Harper & Row, 1973), 168.

[3] Philip Yancey, *What's So Amazing about Grace?* (Grand Rapids.: Zondervan, 1997), 41.

[4] Ibid, 60.

[5] John F. MacArthur, *The Freedom and Power of Forgiveness* (Wheaton: Crossway, 1998), 113-4.

Unit Two

The Case Against Forgiveness

Can you recall ever hearing a respected spiritual advisor say to a crime or abuse victim: "What happened to you is so awful that you would be a fool to forgive. A lifetime of bitterness is your only reasonable response"? That's what I thought. You've probably never heard a good case against forgiveness. The following story makes that case if any story can.

Simon Wiesenthal was a Jewish architect incarcerated in a Nazi concentration camp during World War II. One day Wiesenthal was on a work detail in a local hospital where German soldiers were treated. A nurse ordered him to follow her to a patient's room. There Wiesenthal found a young SS trooper named Karl whose head was wrapped in bandages. He gripped Wiesenthal's hand and explained that before he died, he had a confession that must be made to a Jew.

Karl told Simon that on the Russian front he had fought in a village where 200 Jews were captured. Karl's squad was ordered to plant cans of gasoline in a vacant house, then herd the Jewish men, women, and children inside. They were instructed to ignite the gasoline and shoot anyone who attempted to flee.

The prisoners were packed so tightly into the house that they could barely move. The soldiers threw grenades through the windows and the house erupted in flames. Karl recalled looking up through a second-floor window to see a man whose clothing was on fire. He held a small child in his arms and a woman stood beside him. With his free hand the man covered the child's eyes, then jumped to the street. Seconds later, the mother followed. But Karl and his fellow soldiers obeyed their orders.

"We shot," he groaned. "Oh, God ... I shall never forget ... it still haunts me." Karl continued: "I know that what I have told you is terrible. I have longed to talk about it to a Jew and beg forgiveness from him. I know that what I am asking is almost too much, but without your answer I cannot die in peace."

In his book *The Sunflower,* Wiesenthal recalled his response: "I stood up and looked in his direction at his folded hands. At last I made up my mind and without a word I left the room."

Through the remainder of his life, Wiesenthal struggled with his decision. Should he have forgiven the repentant Nazi, or are some crimes too heinous to be forgiven? Wiesenthal ended the story by asking his readers, "What would you have done?"[1]

666

What would have been your response in Wiesenthal's place?

_____

If the answer "forgive" comes a little too easily, imagine that the person confessing to you is detailing the murder of your children, not those of a stranger. Now what would you say?

Do some offenses fall outside the circle of grace?
❑ Yes ❑ No ❑ I'm not sure

Are some wrongs impossible to absolve through the simple apology, "I'm sorry. Please forgive me"? ❑ Yes ❑ No
❑ I'm not sure

Is forgiveness sometimes too much to ask from a hurting victim? ❑ Yes ❑ No ❑ I'm not sure

I believe Wiesenthal's story illustrates and underscores the four most logical arguments against forgiveness.

1. Forgiveness denies the seriousness of sin. "If I forgive, it's the same as saying that the offender's wrong actions don't really matter." The truth is, some offenses are so petty that we should overlook them—a forgotten birthday, an interrupted sentence, an unreturned phone call. Read Solomon's wise counsel in the margin.

Certainly small slights are painful at times. But, as Solomon explained, a wise person is one who doesn't make a federal case out of every injury in life. Instead, he soothes his hurt with the gracious understanding that everyone makes mistakes.

However, is it wise to treat every offense in that manner? If I counsel a mother to overlook the sexual abuse she suffered as a child in the same way I suggest a friend overlook a coworker's sarcastic remark, then I trivialize her pain and minimize the seriousness of incest.

Some offenses are so serious that they cannot be overlooked any more than God can overlook our sin. It's impossible for God to excuse sin. One of the great misconceptions about salvation is that God tells us, "What you did was bad, but I love you so much that we'll forget this ever happened." A holy God is incapable of such an action.

"Starting a quarrel is like breaching a dam; so drop the matter before a dispute breaks out."
Proverbs 17:14

"A man's wisdom gives him patience; it is to his glory to overlook an offense."
Proverbs 19:11

The verses in the margin remind us of the truth that God's mercy cannot override His holiness. Offenses demand payment. If a perfect God finds it impossible to summarily dismiss sin against Him, how do we think we'll overlook the serious hurts inflicted by others? Sin creates an obligation, and someone has to pay. Whatever forgiveness is, it should not be confused with glossing over the seriousness of a wrong. People also complain that …

2. Forgiveness lets people off the hook too easily. A basic hindrance to forgiveness is the fear of further abuse. We fear that forgiving our offenders gives them permission to hurt us again, and even more deeply.

"Have nothing to do with a false charge and do not put an innocent or honest person to death, for I will not acquit the guilty."
Exodus 23:7

Describe an example from your experience in which fear of further abuse or hurt hampered forgiveness.

_____

Such a legitimate fear about the consequences of forgiveness may have prompted Peter to ask Jesus: "Lord, how many times shall I forgive my brother when he sins against me? Up to seven times?" (Matt. 18:21).

An automatic response might be: "Peter, don't be stupid. You know there's no limit to forgiveness!" But before you judge Peter, ask yourself, "How many times am I willing to forgive a person for committing the same serious offense against me?"

'The Lord is slow to anger and great in power; the Lord will not leave the guilty unpunished."
Nahum 1:3

Record that number and explain your answer.

_____

_____

Suddenly, Peter's offer of seven times seems quite generous. This is especially true given the culture in which Peter lived. A popular rabbi of the day taught that you forgave people three times, but the fourth time you refused. Peter was offering more than twice the going rate of grace, but he still believed there must be some limit to forgiveness to prevent offenders from taking advantage. To be honest, most of us probably believe the same way. We could also cite a third argument against forgiveness.

3. Forgiveness places too much responsibility on the victim. One counseling office gave the following advice to victims of incest:

> Dear Victim:
> If you are like most victims who have been sexually abused, you are asking many questions of yourself. We have all heard the old favorites from sex offenders, family members, ministers, and clergy, "Forgive and forget; let bygones be bygones; let's bury the hatchet and start over." These statements seem to encourage victims to feel as though it is their responsibility to take action regarding resolution and forgiveness. This seems strange since victims are innocent and not responsible for what has occurred.... We believe you as a victim are innocent, and we demand restitution be paid to you in some form. You will learn that your rehabilitation is our goal. You are not responsible for the sexual abuse, and you are not responsible for forgiveness. Your sexual offender is responsible for both these things....[2]

Not only is it unfair to place the forgiveness burden on a victim, some say, but it's also unrealistic. Is it logical to expect an incest victim ever to forget what happened to her? Can a spouse simply press a delete key and remove from memory the pain of an adulterous mate? Should an employee, unfairly terminated six months before eligibility for his or her pension, be expected to conclude, "What happened to me was bad, but I'll get over it"?

Respond to this question: When we ask people to let go of such serious hurts, are we asking them to do the impossible?

Remember that God doesn't exempt us from tasks just because they're unfair or difficult. For example, consider Jesus' famous words from the Sermon on the Mount:

> You have heard that it was said, "Eye for eye, and tooth for tooth." But I tell you, Do not resist an evil person. If someone strikes you on the right cheek, turn to him the other also. And

if someone wants to sue you and take your tunic, let him have your cloak as well. If someone forces you to go one mile, go with him two miles (Matt. 5:38-41).

Notice that in each situation Jesus mentioned, He placed responsibility on the offended, not on the offender. The offended is to turn the other cheek, offer his coat as well as his shirt, and walk the second mile.

4. Forgiveness is unjust. We are all created in the image of God and, regardless of how badly that image has been marred, we still retain a residue of innate fairness. When we observe a wrong being committed, we understand it's unjust for that wrong to go unpunished.

In Dostoevsky's *The Brothers Karamazov,* one of the characters relates to his brother the following incident. A landlord was irritated by a small boy who kept throwing rocks at his dogs. To teach the village peasants to respect his property, the landlord forced the little boy's mother to watch while he loosed a pack of dogs on her son. The dogs tore the boy's body into bloody pieces while the mother looked on in horror.[3]

Could the landlord ever be forgiven for such a wicked action? Who would be in a position to forgive the landlord? And if, by some miracle, the mother of the murdered boy could find it in her heart to forgive the landlord, wouldn't there still be something fundamentally unfair in allowing the landlord to go free without any consequences?

List again the four arguments against forgiveness:

1. _____

2. _____

3. _____

4. _____

Based on your life experiences, which of these arguments is the most convincing? Explain your answer.

_____

_____

Understanding Forgiveness

These four objections result from a basic misunderstanding of the concept of forgiveness. Before we define the word, let's understand what forgiveness is not. First, forgiveness is not denying the reality of our pain. To demand that someone simply forget a wrong is like asking a man who has lost both arms to pass the ketchup. He can't do it!

Second, forgiveness is not letting our offender off the hook. Even when we choose to forgive, such forgiveness does not necessarily erase the consequences of our offender's actions. Justice may be necessary in spite of our forgiveness.

Third, forgiveness is not unfair. To forgive another person does not necessitate violating some cosmic rule of justice requiring that every offense must be punished. Requiring us to do something unfair would violate God's nature. "Is God unfair?" the apostle Paul exclaimed. "Not at all!" (Rom. 9:14).

Recap the three statements, explaining what forgiveness is not by completing the open-ended statements following each one.

1. Forgiveness is not denying the reality of our pain means ...

_____

2. Forgiveness is not letting our offender off the hook means ...

_____

3. Forgiveness is not unfair means ...

_____

If forgiveness is none of the above, then what is it? The Greek word translated *forgive* carries the idea of a release from some type of an obligation, such as release from a marriage or a job, and most commonly, release from a financial obligation. That's how Jesus illustrated the concept of forgiveness with Simon the Pharisee during his dinner party (see unit one). "A certain moneylender had two debtors ...," the illustration began. The moneylender chose to release both of the debtors from their very real obligations. The money owed was not a figment of the lender's imagination.

Notice that in both cases:

1. The lender had a legal right to be repaid.
2. The borrowers had an obligation to pay.
3. There was a deficit between the borrowers' debt and resources.

Nowhere in Jesus' brief example is there an indication that the lender was unreasonable in his expectation to be repaid. Although the borrowers could not repay their debts, the lender was the innocent party in this situation. Good accounting demanded that the books be balanced. Debts on record had to be satisfied by someone.

Perhaps the greatest misunderstanding about forgiveness is that it simply overlooks another's transgression. Just as God is incapable of sweeping our sin under some divine doormat, so it is impossible to excuse the serious wrongs of others. The truth is that someone always has to pay because an offense always creates an obligation that must be satisfied.

Imagine that you're stopped at a red light and BAM!—someone rear-ends you. Startled, you get out of the car and inspect the damage. Fortunately, nothing seems to be seriously wrong with your car. The other driver pours out his apologies, offering the name of his insurance agent. Feeling especially magnanimous, you say, "Forget it," and drive off. You have overlooked his offense.

The next day you notice a rattle in the rear end of your car and feel your car pulling strongly to the right. You take the car to your local garage and the mechanic informs you that yesterday's accident inflicted $2000 worth of damage to your car.

Who is going to pay for the repairs? Not the driver you let off the hook. Not the mechanic—he isn't prone to doing charity work. The only person left to pay is you! The offense (being rear-ended) created an obligation (the cost of repairing the car) that had to be satisfied.

Now let's revise the story. After the impact, you immediately notice a huge dent in your rear bumper. You realize it will cost big bucks to repair the damage. But this time the driver is a little old lady in tears over the accident. Between sobs she explains that she's a retired missionary with limited resources and no insurance. "What am I going to do?" she laments. You tell her to forget it; you will take care of the damage.

Again, the mechanic informs you that it will cost $2,000 to repair the car so you decide to cover the deficit yourself. Here again, the financial obligation did not suddenly evaporate. The mechanic did not say: "Oh, it was a missionary who hit you? Well, then, forget it. I'll be happy to fix your car for free." An obligation remained that you willingly covered. The story illustrates the essence of forgiveness. When we forgive:

1. We acknowledge a wrong has occurred.
2. We recognize that the wrong has created an obligation for repayment.
3. We choose to release our offender from that obligation and to cover the loss ourselves.

Beside the three statements above, rank them as "E"–easiest to do; "N"–not so easy to do"; or "H"–hard to do. What does this exercise tell you about your forgiveness attitudes and habits?

_____

_____

Most of us have little problem recalling and recounting indignantly the wrongs against us. We are excellent record keepers and can calculate precisely how much someone owes us for his or her offense against us. The stumbling point for most of us is the third ingredient of forgiveness.

Why should we release someone from an obligation to us and suffer the consequences ourselves? Record your initial thoughts in the margin; look back at what you've written after you've read the following section, "The Case for Forgiveness."

The Case for Forgiveness

So far we've explored some very logical arguments against forgiveness. Do equally convincing reasons prompt us to unilaterally forgive another person? When everyone around us and everything inside us tells us to cling to a wrong until the offender "pays in full," why should we suddenly let go of his obligation?

Jesus anticipated such objections. When Peter was voluntarily raising the forgiveness limit to seven (and feeling rather self-righteous about it, I'm sure), Jesus astounded him by saying, "I tell you, not seven times, but seventy-seven times" (Matt. 18:22). Jesus then told a dramatic story related in Matthew 18:23-34. Here's the *Reader's Digest* version:

A king, suffering a serious cash-flow problem, decided to call in his accounts receivable. He logically began with the person who owed him the most, a slave with a debt of "10 thousand talents." Since a single talent represented 60 to 80 pounds of silver or gold, we're talking about upwards of $5,000,000,000 in today's currency. You can only imagine the terror the slave felt when the king said, "Pay up!"

Though the slave couldn't even begin to pay such a debt, he offered to repay everything. Can you imagine a more pitiful sight than his begging for just a little more time to repay a $5,000,000,000 debt? With uncharacteristic mercy, the king felt compassion for the slave and released him from his debt.

In the opening scene, we observe a perfect illustration of forgiveness. The slave owed a very real debt. The king had every right to expect payment. But the king voluntarily released the slave from his obligation and covered the loss of the canceled obligation himself. Why? Jesus said the king felt *compassion*. Perhaps he put himself in the slave's sandals, or perhaps he remembered when someone extended grace to him. Let me offer some other strong reasons for choosing forgiveness.

1. Forgiveness Is Often the Only Way to Settle a Debt

The slave owed a debt he could never pay. What alternatives could the king consider? "Well," you say, "he didn't have to release the slave; he could have imprisoned him. That would have been a just punishment." But would the slave's imprisonment have put even one dollar in the king's coffers? Was there any advantage to demanding that the slave remain behind bars for the rest of his life? The king was astute and realized that he was holding an uncollectible account receivable. No matter how much the slave suffered, the king was going to take a financial bath.

Many people are struggling with forgiveness because they are unaware that the "debt" they hold is really worthless. They mistakenly believe some payment can be extracted from their offenders that will compensate for their loss. Understandably, they want vengeance. But the truth is that very few sinners have the resources to pay for their offenses. What satisfactory payment could someone offer you to compensate for:
  • a child killed by a drunk driver?
  • a reputation slandered by a false rumor?
  • a marriage destroyed by infidelity?
  • an innocent childhood stolen by an immoral relative?

Some would argue that the offender's suffering as a result of suitable punishment helps to compensate the victim. If the offense cannot be compensated, then the suffering must be matched.

Take a moment to argue in favor of this position. How would you defend the "rightness" of this view?

_____

_____

Consider Gandhi's observation: "An eye for an eye, a tooth for a tooth cannot sustain itself forever; ultimately both parties end up blind and toothless."[4]

At first glance, Jesus' solution appears outlandish, but on closer examination seems more reasonable: "You have heard that it was said, 'Eye for eye, and tooth for tooth.' But I tell you, Do not resist an evil person. If someone strikes you on the right cheek, turn to him the other also" (Matt. 5:38-39).

Like the king in the parable, Jesus understood that sometimes forgiveness is the only way to break the endless cycle of hurts and unfairness, especially in situations where an offender can never make satisfactory payment for his wrongdoings.

Reread your argument above. In light of Jesus' words in Matthew 5:38-39, how might you amend your stance?

_____

_____

2. Forgiveness Frees Us to Get On with Life

I've made several financial mistakes in my life, but the greatest was partnering in business with friends. A good friend once presented me with a "spectacular opportunity" to double my money within six months. I jumped on board and invested a rather large amount in his venture. As you might have predicted, the deal did not deliver what my friend promised. Feeling badly about the situation, he promised to return my money "in a week." A week passed and I received no check. Two weeks, still no money. Whenever I dropped by his office, he was always in a meeting. My phone calls went unreturned. For six months, I anxiously checked the mail for the promised check.

Suddenly I realized I was more concerned about my friend's obligation than he was. I recalled comedian Buddy Hackett's comment: "I've had a few arguments with people, but I never carry a grudge. You know why? While you're carrying a grudge, they're out dancing."

I began to ask myself, "Why do I want to be a financial and emotional hostage to this guy?" So I called my friend and said: "I know you've been avoiding me for months. I understand that you're probably in no position to pay me back the money. So as far as I'm concerned, you don't owe me anything. Let's rebuild our friendship."

Admittedly, my motivation was primarily selfish. I was ready to get on with my life, freed from my daily mailbox vigil.

The king in Jesus' parable may have had a similar motivation to forgive. He had too many responsibilities running a kingdom to allow himself to be distracted. If the king was always checking with the royal bookkeeper on the slave's debt, he risked neglecting more pressing duties. Since the slave could never pay the debt anyway, why not cut his losses rather than risk needless preoccupation with a hopeless situation?

One of the best reasons for forgiving someone is not what it does for them, but what it does for us. Letting go of a rattlesnake might help the snake, but it benefits you as well. I realize that such an argument for forgiveness seems self-serving.

One of the best reasons for forgiving someone is not what it does for them, but what it does for us.

🔥

For the sake of argument, how does not risking "needless pre-occupation with a hopeless situation" help you? Record the benefits here:

_____

_____

Remember—God's Word tells us to free ourselves from anything that distracts us from serving Christ:

"Therefore, since we are surrounded by such a great cloud of witnesses, let us throw off everything that hinders and the sin that so easily entangles, and let us run with perseverance the race marked out for us. Let us fix our eyes on Jesus, the author and perfecter of our faith" (Heb. 12:1-2).

Think this question through one more time. What sins might you commit by remaining focused on the offenses committed against you? Record those sins below.

Pause and pray about what you've just written. Are you willing to ask forgiveness for the sins you've just confessed?

3. Forgiveness Is an Antidote to Needless Suffering

In the opening scene of the Bible example, the king was the central character. However, Jesus shifted His audience's attention to the unforgiving slave. Imagine the relief that slave must have felt as he left the palace realizing his $5,000,000,000 burden had just been lifted. I'm sure he repeatedly shouted the king's words: "You are forgiven. You are forgiven. You are forgiven!"

Unbelievably, a wild thought entered his mind. "Debt? Money? Come to think of it, someone owes me some money, too." A fellow slave owed him about $16 in today's currency. So he sought him out and demanded repayment. "I don't have the money right now, but if you're patient, I'll repay you," the friend promised.

These are exactly the words the first slave had spoken to the king. But unlike the king, the slave had no compassion on his fellow slave. He "had the man thrown into prison until he could pay the debt" (Matt. 18:30).

When the king heard what the forgiven slave had done, he was outraged. How could someone who had been forgiven so much refuse to forgive so little? The king, "in anger ... turned him over to the jailers to be tortured, until he should pay back all he owed" (Matt. 18:34).

Then Jesus added the zinger: "This is how my heavenly Father will treat each of you unless you forgive your brother from your heart" (Matt. 18:35). Strong words. Is Jesus teaching that God is some sadist who enjoys inflicting pain on His children who refuse to forgive? Of course not. But those who refuse to forgive enter their own private torture chamber. They sentence themselves to a lifetime of needless pain.

In *The Freedom and Power of Forgiveness,* John MacArthur vividly describes the results of unforgiveness:

Unforgiveness is a toxin. It poisons the heart and mind with bitterness, distorting one's whole perspective on life. Anger, resentment, and sorrow begin to overshadow and overwhelm the unforgiving person — a kind of soul-pollution that enflames evil appetites and evil emotions.[5]

What experience have you had with the poison of bitterness? Describe the state of your mind, soul, and body when you've harbored bitterness over some situation or someone.

_____

_____

The Bible's term for _unforgiveness_ is _bitterness_. The Greek word translated _bitter_ comes from a word meaning "sharp" or "pointed." Just as there are certain tastes and smells that are "sharp" to the senses, all of us can recall past offenses that still hurt us when we remember them. Those who refuse to let go of offenses risk poisoning their own lives and the lives of others around them. That is why the writer of Hebrews warned: "See to it that no one misses the grace of God and that no bitter root grows up to cause trouble and defile many" (Heb. 12:15).

With every offense comes a choice. Through God's supernatural power, we can release the offense and become _better_, or we can hold on to that offense and become _bitter_. The choice is ours. Letting go promotes healing; holding on ensures infection.

James Garfield had been president of the United States for less than four months when he was shot in the back on July 2, 1881. While the president remained conscious, the doctor probed the wound with his little finger, unsuccessfully trying to detect the bullet. Over the course of the summer, teams of doctors tried to locate the bullet. The president clung to life through July and August, but in September he finally died—not from the gunshot wound, but from infection. The repeated probing of the wound, which the doctor thought would help the president, ultimately killed him.[6]

Continually reliving our hurts infects not only our lives, but also the lives of those around us. One of the strongest arguments for forgiveness is considering the consequences of unforgiveness. Frederick Buechner has written:

Of the Seven Deadly Sins, anger is possibly the most fun. To lick your wounds, to smack your lips over grievances long past, to roll over your tongue the prospect of bitter confrontations still to come, to savor to the last toothsome morsel both the pain you are given and the pain you are giving back — in many ways it is a feast fit for a king. The chief drawback is that what you are wolfing down is yourself. The skeleton at the feast is you.[7]

4. Forgiveness Is the Obligation of the Forgiven

Throughout the Bible an inseparable link seems to exist between receiving and granting forgiveness. In Jesus' story, even the other pagan slaves realized that link. They were astounded that someone who had been forgiven so much would refuse to forgive so little, and it was by their report that the king learned about the first slave's refusal to forgive.

When we read this parable, it's apparent that the king represents God and the first slave represents us. The Bible teaches that our sin against God has produced an obligation we could never hope to repay. Trying to pay for our sin through good works or religious ritual is just as futile as a slave trying to repay a $5,000,000,000 debt! It's not possible. But just as the king was moved with compassion by the slave's predicament, God was moved by our hopeless situation and sent Christ to die for us.

The interaction between the two slaves represents our relationship to those who wrong us. The first slave had every right to collect his $16. No court would argue otherwise. But Jesus' point was that the first slave had an obligation to release his friend from his debt, because he had just been freed from a greater debt. Forgiveness is the obligation of the forgiven.

Perhaps somewhere in your past there's a hurtful experience from which you haven't fully recovered. It may be abandonment by a mate, the betrayal of a friend, or injury inflicted by a stranger. I don't want to discount for even a moment the reality of your anguish. But listen carefully to what Jesus said in this story. While the pain you've experienced is real, it is also negligible compared to the wrong you have committed against God. The difference between another person's sin against you and your sin against God is the difference between $16 and $5,000,000,000! Forgiveness is the obligation of the forgiven.

Forgiveness is the obligation of the forgiven.

The difference between another person's sin against you and your sin against God is the difference between $16 and $5,000,000,000.

In this unit you've studied four arguments against and four arguments in favor of forgiveness. On the following chart, summarize the cases for and against forgiveness.

The Case for Forgiveness   The Case Against Forgiveness

_____   _____

_____   _____

_____   _____

_____   _____

On the continuum below, put an **F** at the point that best
represents your feelings about forgiveness, an **A** at the point
that best represents your attitudes about forgiveness, and a **B** at
the point that best represents your behavior of forgiveness.

For	*Against*

What have you learned about yourself from the positioning of
these three marks?

_____

_____

_____

---

[1] Lewis Smedes, *Forgive & Forget* (New York: HarperCollins, 1996), 126-7.

[2] Jane Hindman, as quoted in Robert Jeffress, *Choose Your Attitudes, Change Your Life* (Wheaton, Ill.: Victor, 1992), 100-1.

[3] Smedes, 88.

[4] Yancey, *What's So Amazing About Grace?* (Zondervan, 1997), 55.

[5] MacArthur, *The Freedom and Power of Forgiveness,* 161.

[6] http://home.nycap.rr.com/useless/garfield/garfield.html.

[7] Frederick Buechner, *Wishful Thinking: A Seeker's ABC* (1973; reprint, revised and expanded, San Francisco: HarperSanFrancisco, 1993), 2.

PART TWO

Removing the Barriers to Forgiveness

Marla's family recently moved to a different town. She was concerned about her children making new friends. Marla did all she could to foster good relationships with other mothers in her neighborhood. She even told them about her children's difficulties in finding new friends.

One day Marla learned those same mothers had organized a slumber party and invited most of the neighborhood children—except hers. First she was hurt, but the hurt soon turned to anger. How could a group of mothers be so cruel, when they knew how painful the experience would be to her children? Marla wrestled with whether or not to confront the women and risk being further ostracized or to let it go. Could she honestly forgive these women without first hearing the words, "I'm sorry"?

Clint hated confrontations, but he knew he must talk to his partner Jason about yesterday's blow-up in front of the other employees. Clint was totally unprepared for his partner's response. Jason almost screamed: "Just who do you think you are, talking to me that way? We're equal partners, and if I have a problem, I'll talk to you any way I want, any time I want. As for the other employees, forget them! I don't work for them; they work for me!"

Clint's priority was to get on with operating the company, but could he forgive Jason, who refused to acknowledge a serious mistake? Even if he was able to forgive Jason, could their relationship ever be salvaged?

Sara wrestled for years with the guilt and pain of an incestuous relationship with her uncle. It began when she was five and continued through her early teen years. Divorced twice, Sara has been in therapy for as long as she can remember. In a sermon series on the topic of forgiveness, her pastor shared three ingredients necessary to initiate a "forgiveness transaction":

1. Offender and offended acknowledge that a wrong has occurred.
2. The offender repents of his sin.
3. The offended party releases the offender of his obligation.

This approach made sense to Sara except for one problem: her uncle was dead. How can a dead person acknowledge a wrong or repent of his sin? Are Sara's chances for emotional healing doomed by the fact that her uncle died without ever asking her forgiveness?

Unit Three

Saying and Hearing "I'm Sorry"

The three examples you just read illustrate a frequently cited barrier to forgiveness: the need for repentance. Is repentance a requirement for granting forgiveness to others? Can you honestly and effectively forgive someone who is unaware or unconcerned about the offense? What if they are unwilling to admit to the offense or unable to ask forgiveness because of illness or death? The forgiveness "experts" are divided on this issue. Let's consider several arguments against unilateral forgiving.

First, some say Luke 17:3 shows Jesus didn't teach unconditional forgiveness. Those who oppose unilateral forgiving say God demands conditions be met before forgiving, and we are to follow God's example. They offer at least three powerful arguments for demanding repentance before granting forgiveness. As you read the points below, notice that to each one I've offered a counterpoint worth considering.

"So watch yourselves. If your brother sins, rebuke him, and if he repents, forgive him."
Luke 17:3

1. Forgiveness Needs to Be Earned

Do you agree or disagree? ❏ **Agree** ❏ **Disagree**

What particular experiences or encounters in your past influence your answer today?

_____

POINT—When someone injures us (so this argument goes), they have created a cosmic debt that somehow must be satisfied. To offer forgiveness to an unrepentant person is fundamentally unfair.

Consider the prodigal son (see Luke 15:11-32). The father wanted to forgive the son. But before he could welcome the son back into the family (some people claim), he first had to hear the words, "Father, I have sinned"—evidence, we're told, that forgiveness must be earned.

COUNTERPOINT—The biggest problem with this argument is there's always a deficit between what our offender owes us and what, in fact, he can pay. In the parable of the unforgiving slave, a tremendous disparity stood between the slave's debt and his resources. Although the slave begged for mercy and promised to repay everything, the debt was too large for him to erase in a thousand lifetimes, much less one.

"For it is by grace you have been saved, through faith—and this not from yourselves, it is the gift of God—not by works, so that no one can boast."
Ephesians 2:8-9

Those who demand repentance before granting forgiveness are operating under the illusion that somehow their offender's repentance will be sufficient to cover the offense. The words "I'm sorry" may be powerful enough to bring momentary relief to a wound, but they are insufficient in themselves to effect permanent healing.

Isn't this true in our relationship with God? Could we ever do anything to earn God's forgiveness? Is saying "I'm sorry" enough to erase the stain of our sin?

How silly (and prideful) it is to think that we could ever repay our Creator for the hurt we have inflicted upon Him by any act of penitence, much less uttering a simple "I'm sorry." Mark it, circle it, and remember this truth forever: We are not saved by our repentance but by God's grace. Repentance plays a vital role in the forgiveness process, but repentance is powerless in and of itself to secure forgiveness.

State in your own words the first argument for and against demanding repentance before granting forgiveness:

For: _____

Against: _____

Re-examine your initial response to the argument for demanding repentance (p. 35). How would you change your answer now, if at all?

_____

Those arguing against unilateral forgiveness present a second reason.

2. Forgiving an Unrepentant Person Invites Further Abuse

Do you agree or disagree? ❑ Agree ❑ Disagree

What particular experiences or encounters in your past influence your answer today?

_____

POINT—If a woman forgives her philandering husband before he expresses any remorse, isn't she in effect wearing a "Kick Me" sign? By forgiving without at least insisting on a "Please forgive me," aren't we doing a fundamental disservice to both the offender as well as society?

Your teenager breaks a curfew. You confront him, but he expresses no remorse. What do you do? You could say that you forgive him and hope it never happens again. But unless he expresses genuine sorrow for what he's done, aren't you accommodating further rule-breaking?

Forgiveness can be dangerous business. Grace without repentance risks further abuse. The apostle Paul recognized the potential abuse of grace. After stating the truth that "where sin increased, grace increased all the more," he asked: "What shall we say, then? Shall we go on sinning so that grace may increase?" (Rom. 5:20; 6:1).

COUNTERPOINT—In fairness to the apostle Paul, we should allow him to answer his own question. He said: "By no means! We died to sin; how can we live in it any longer?" (Rom. 6:2). To Paul, it was unthinkable that a forgiven person who had been freed from the power of sin would ever voluntarily choose to become a servant of sin again. I love the way Max Lucado illustrates the absurdity of such a decision:

> Most of my life I've been a closet slob. I was slow to see the logic of neatness. ... Then I got married. Denalyn was so patient. She said she didn't mind my habits ... if I didn't mind sleeping outside. Since I did, I began to change. ... By the time Denalyn's parents came to visit, I was a new man. I could go three days without throwing a sock behind the couch.
>
> Then came the moment of truth. Denalyn went out of town for a week. Initially I reverted to the old man. I figured I'd be a slob for six days and clean on the seventh. But something strange happened, a curious discomfort. I couldn't relax with dirty dishes in the sink. When I saw an empty potato chip sack on the floor I—hang on to your hat—bent over and picked it up! I actually put my bath towel back on the rack. What had happened to me?
>
> Simple. I'd been exposed to a higher standard.[1]

Max's experience is the essence of Paul's argument in the remainder of Romans 6. Though the downside of God's forgiveness is that it invites further abuse, the benefit of forgiveness is that it exposes us to a higher way of living, so that, as Paul put it, "we too may live a new life" (v. 4).

ƦƦƦ

State in your own words the second argument for and against demanding repentance before granting forgiveness:

For: _____

Against: _____

Re-examine your initial response to the argument for demanding repentance (p. 36). How would you change your answer now, if at all?

_____

Receiving forgiveness should motivate us to change, but it doesn't always. Forgiving an unrepentant person can give license to further abuses. Those who teach conditional forgiveness also pose a third reason.

3. Forgiving an Unrepentant Person Is Unscriptural

Do you agree or disagree? ❑ Agree ❑ Disagree
What particular experiences or encounters in your past influence your answer today?

_____

POINT—The strongest argument for demanding repentance before offering forgiveness is that the Bible seems to require it. Look at some of the scriptural evidence. First, repentance appears to be a condition for receiving God's forgiveness. Second, repentance also appears to be a condition for granting forgiveness to others.

The heart of the argument is really quite simple. If (a) God requires us to acknowledge our sin before He forgives us, and (b) we are to forgive others in the same way God has forgiven us, then it seems to follow naturally that (c) we should require our offender to repent before we forgive him or her.

COUNTERPOINT—It's a logical conclusion, but it fails to note an important distinction—the difference between receiving forgiveness and granting forgiveness. The issue of repentance is vitally important to accepting forgiveness, but irrelevant to giving forgiveness. When you address the subject of repentance, know first to whom you are speaking: the offender or the offended.

Perhaps this illustration will help. When a husband informs me that he is contemplating leaving his mate to pursue a more fulfilling relationship, it would be inappropriate for me to give him a copy of my book, *Guilt-Free Living*, to soothe his inevitable pangs of remorse. Instead, I should advise him that God hates divorce and remind him of the sanctity of marriage.

However, if I'm counseling someone who has already divorced and remarried, my advice would differ. I would talk to that person about receiving God's grace and resolving to build a strong marriage.

Similarly, in discussing the relationship between repentance and forgiveness, first determine: Am I speaking to the offender or the offended? If someone says, "I want my mate to forgive me for this or that," then the issue of repentance is vitally important. But if the wounded party says, "I'm having difficulty forgiving my mate because he shows no remorse," then repentance is less important.

State in your own words the third argument for and against demanding repentance before granting forgiveness:

For: _____

Against: _____

Re-examine your initial response to the argument for demanding repentance (p. 38). How would you change your answer now, if at all?

_____

Review the three point/counterpoint arguments once again. Then determine:

If I'm in need of forgiveness, then I favor the point/counterpoint (circle an answer).

If I'm deciding whether or not to forgive another, then I favor the point/counterpoint (circle an answer).

What do you learn about yourself from your answers?

_____

The Greek word translated *repent* comes from a root word meaning "to change one's mind." It is a change of mind that leads to a change of direction. In the following four instances, repentance is vital.

1. Repentance Is Essential to Receiving God's Forgiveness

Although God's grace is the basis for salvation, repentance is the channel through which that grace is received. First John offers a general principle about God's forgiveness that applies to everyone: "If we claim to be without sin, we deceive ourselves, and the truth is not in us. If we confess our sins, he is faithful and just and will forgive us our sins and purify us from all unrighteousness" (1 John 1:8-9). Repentance is a prerequisite for receiving God's forgiveness.

2. Repentance Is Essential to Reconciliation

While God requires me to unconditionally forgive the business partner who cheats me, He does not require that I remain in business with him. Repentance is necessary to rebuild a broken relationship with another person and with God.

3. Repentance Is Essential to Restoration to a Position

In Matthew 18, Jesus discussed two types of offenses: personal offenses and corporate offenses. In that chapter, Peter asked: "Lord, how many times shall I forgive my brother when he sins against me? Up to seven times?" (v. 21). Jesus answered Peter's question with the parable about the unforgiving slave, illustrating the unlimited, unilateral, and unconditional nature of forgiveness on the personal level.

But how are we to respond to the sinning church member whose lifestyle is the talk of the community? In Matthew 18:15-20, Jesus discussed a procedure for restoring those who have fallen into sin—a procedure that demands repentance.

4. Repentance Is Essential to Relief from Guilt

Guilt is an indicator that something in our life is wrong. Unfortunately, some people try to prematurely extinguish their guilt by denial or rationalization. King David tried that approach for about six months after one particular sin—and it was wholly ineffective:

"When I kept silent,
my bones wasted away
through my groaning all day long.
For day and night
your hand was heavy upon me;
my strength was sapped
as in the heat of summer" (Ps. 32:3-4).

Only when David repented did he experience relief from guilt:

"Then I acknowledged my sin to you
and did not cover up my iniquity.
I said, 'I will confess
my transgressions to the Lord'—
and you forgave
the guilt of my sin" (Ps. 32:5).

Recall and review the four instances just discussed and fill in the blanks below. Repentance is essential to:

1. _____ God's _____

2. _____ (with other _____ we have wronged)

3. _____ to a _____

4. _____ from _____

Now let me speak to the one who must choose whether to forgive, the one asking, "Can I honestly release others from their obligations to me without first demanding their repentance?" Allow me to briefly make the case for unconditionally forgiving an unrepentant offender.

1. Unconditional Forgiveness Is Biblical

In some instances the Bible demands repentance, but forgiveness—releasing someone of his obligation to us for the wrong committed against us—takes place solely in our own hearts. Consider Jesus' words as He applied the parable of the unforgiving slave: "This is how my heavenly Father will treat each of you unless you forgive your brother from your heart" (Matt. 18:35).

In the Hebrew world, the heart represented a person's mind. For example, the psalmist wrote, "The fool says in his heart, 'There is no God' " (Ps. 14:1). Proverbs observes, "For as he thinketh in his heart, so is he" (Prov. 23:7, KJV). Knowing this helps us understand Jesus' words. The command to forgive "from your heart," implies that forgiveness is a rational choice I make independently of what others may or may not do.

Jesus again illustrated the unconditional nature of forgiveness in His instructions about prayer: "And when you stand praying, if you hold anything against anyone, forgive him, so that your Father in heaven may forgive you your sins" (Mark 11:25).

Understand the scenario Jesus described here. You have set your alarm clock 20 minutes early to spend time with God in prayer. As you review your lists of requests, a stray thought enters your mind—some hateful words that your mate yelled at you several weeks earlier. Instead of confronting your spouse, you chalked it up to a bad day and congratulated yourself on letting it pass without World War III erupting. Now as you attempt to talk with your Heavenly Father, your mate's words drift back into your mind. What should you do? Some would misapply Matthew 5:24 ("first go and be reconciled to your brother; then come and offer your gift") to say that you should seek restoration with your mate before continuing to pray.

Jesus had a more radical idea: "Forgive." Whether your spouse is in the next room or the next state is irrelevant. You have the capability to let go of that offense in the privacy of your will and mind.

One other thought: What about Jesus' command seems to imply that repentance is a condition for granting forgiveness? Look again at Jesus' words in the margin.

Let's not put words in Jesus' mouth, as some try to do. The verse does not read, "AND IF AND ONLY IF HE REPENTS, forgive him." Nowhere in this verse does Jesus advise withholding forgiveness from a person who refuses to repent. Repentance is our offender's responsibility; forgiveness is our responsibility.

"So watch yourselves. If your brother sins, rebuke him, and if he repents, forgive him."
Luke 17:3

Repentance is our offender's responsibility; forgiveness is our responsibility.

Make a study appointment for yourself during this week. At that time, use your concordance or other Bible study helps to locate verses describing how to forgive or other examples of how people were forgiven. Record what you find.

2. Unconditional Forgiveness Is Practical

Demanding our offender's repentance, remorse, or rehabilitation can be both uncomfortable and impractical. For example, if the other person must repent before we can grant forgiveness, then we must confront every person who wrongs us before we can genuinely forgive. Otherwise, we are doomed to a bitterness-filled life.

Do you really want to spend your entire life demanding repentance from everyone around you? Won't people run for the hills when they see you coming? And more importantly, doesn't such a confrontational lifestyle contradict the essence of Christian love, a love that "keeps no record of wrongs" (1 Cor. 13:5).

Demanding repentance from our offender can also be impractical. What if you've lost track of the person who has wronged you, or your offender is incapacitated by illness or senility? Must you carry their offenses for the rest of your life? I've talked with people who have been hurt by a now dead parent or grandparent. They desperately longed to hear the words, "I'm sorry; please forgive me," so they might begin to heal emotionally, but that person is forever incapable of demonstrating remorse for the sin. Unconditional forgiveness provides a way to let go of wounds by those who are incapable of repentance.

3. Unconditional Forgiveness Is Beneficial

Probably the best reason to forgive unconditionally is the emotional and spiritual healing it brings to our lives. Often the greatest favor we can do for ourselves is to forgive someone else. Have you ever participated in a three-legged race? Ever heard the spectators roar with laughter watching you hobble to the finish line? *If only I could be freed from this guy, I could make better time,* you probably thought, but for better or worse, you two were bound to each other.

When you demand repentance, remorse, or rehabilitation from your offender, you emotionally bind yourself to him. You can travel no farther than he travels. Your progress is limited by his progress. You are doomed to hobble through life together.

Forgiveness provides a way to cut the emotional cord that binds you to your offender. With it, you are saying: "I no longer wish to be emotionally tied to you. Whether or not you repent is now between you and God. I'm ready to move on with my life, and so I release you of any obligation to me." God wants us free of any weight that distracts us from running the race of life. Unconditional forgiveness allows us to "throw off everything that hinders" and live a Christ-honoring life.

> Unconditional forgiveness provides a way to let go of the wounds of the past inflicted by those who are incapable of repentance.

> *"Therefore, since we are surrounded by such a great cloud of witnesses, let us throw off everything that hinders and the sin that so easily entangles, and let us run with perseverance the race marked out for us."*
> *Hebrews 12:1*

◊◊◊

What other word picture or graphics can you offer to illustrate the emotional bondage of demanding repentance? Describe and/or draw your illustration in the margin.

Many believers have employed a simple but profound method to rid themselves of the emotional bondage of old wounds. They have written letters to the persons who hurt them. In the letters they acknowledge the full reality of the wrong and then expressed their forgiveness to the persons. The letters are not to be mailed. They are a means to deal with the reality of the hurt and the need to express forgiveness.

Perhaps God has brought to your mind the name of someone who has wounded you deeply and is unaware—or worse, unmoved—by his or her actions. Maybe this person has been separated from you by distance or even death. Are you tired of living with that hurt from the past? Do you wish to experience freedom? Unconditional forgiveness is biblical, practical, beneficial, and most importantly, possible.

◊◊◊

Pause and pray for a moment. Inquire of God: "Is it time for me to write a letter to someone who offended or abused me?"

If so, are you willing, with God's help, to write that letter now? Take a sheet of paper and simply begin writing. Record all your thoughts, fears, prayers, and decisions. If not, use the sheet of paper to explain your thoughts and feelings right now—just from considering this exercise—and why you're making the choice not to write a letter of forgiveness.

Consequences, Vengeance, and Justice

One of the greatest barriers to forgiveness is the myth that forgiveness automatically frees our offender from any consequences. Such a misunderstanding makes many people hesitant to forgive; it condemns them to a lifetime of unnecessary bitterness.

◊◊◊

Read and respond to the instructions with each of the following three stories.

A wife divorces her husband because of adulterous escapades. She has three small children at home, and her income is insufficient to provide for their growing needs. Her husband is required to pay child support but has become increasingly tardy in his payments. He comes to her begging for mercy. "I know leaving you was wrong, and I'm sorry for the pain I've caused you and the kids. But these support payments are like a noose around my neck and are preventing me from making the new start I need. If you've really forgiven me, please don't make me keep paying for my mistake. Give me a chance for a fresh beginning."

Case Study #1

Imagine you are the ex-wife in the story. Does forgiveness require you to agree to reduce your ex-husband's child support payments? Why?

_____

_____

A church treasurer is caught embezzling funds from the offerings. When confronted by other church leaders, he admits his mistake, publicly confesses his theft, and makes restitution for the stolen funds. By all outward evidence he is a changed man. He desperately desires reinstatement as treasurer, but some leaders reluctantly say, "How do we know he won't do this again?" Others in the congregation argue: "If we've really forgiven him, why must he keep paying for his mistake? True forgiveness releases a person from his or her obligation."

Case Study #2

Suppose the event happened at your church. With which group of leaders would you be identified? Explain your answer.

_____

_____

A woman was sexually abused by her uncle. Though he has never asked for her forgiveness, she has chosen for her own benefit to forgive him. Her aunt suspects that her husband is involved in some type of immorality, though she is unaware of any specifics. She confronts her niece, asking: "I've noticed that you've always been standoffish with Henry. Has he ever offended you in any way?"

Case Study #3

Put yourself in the woman's place. Do you answer your aunt's question, knowing it could lead to the breakup of her marriage and possibly prison for your uncle? Do you deny any impropriety, or do you make another response? Explain.

_____

_____

Each of the case studies illustrates the same dilemma. Review them once again and record your answer to these two questions:

1. Does forgiveness erase the consequences of sin?

_____

2. Have I truly released a person of any obligation to me when I insist that he be held accountable for his actions?

_____

The answer to those questions is found in the important distinction between two words: *vengeance* and *justice*. Vengeance is my desire to see another person suffer for the pain he has caused me. In your lifetime, someone has committed an offense against you.

Read the verses in the margin. Offer at least three truths from these Scriptures to guide your response to this person:

1. _____

2. _____

3. _____

Remember David's predecessor, Saul, who was so jealous of David that he hounded him relentlessly to kill him. Then when Saul was facing defeat by the Philistines, he fell on his own sword. A young Amalekite, eager to find favor with the new king, brought David the news of Saul's death; he was certain that this would bring joy to the king

"Do not gloat when your enemy falls, when he stumbles, do not let your heart rejoice, or the Lord will see and disapprove and turn his wrath away from him."
Proverbs 24:17-18

"You have heard that it was said, 'eye for eye, and tooth for tooth.' But I tell you, do not resist an evil person. If someone strikes you on the right cheek, turn to him the other also."
Matthew 5:38-39

"Do not take revenge, my friends, but leave room for God's wrath, for it is written, 'It is mine to avenge; I will repay,' says the Lord."
Romans 12:19

and perhaps a cabinet position in the new administration for him. When David asked for an explanation, the young soldier embellished the details of Saul's death to provide himself a more significant role.

&&&

Read this conversation in 2 Samuel 1:6,9-10. Imagine you've been hounded by such a rival. You read his obituary in the newspaper. What would be your first response:

_____

_____

Now in 2 Samuel 1:11-16 read David's reaction. Place an X on the continuum below to rate the similarity of your response.

Unlike David	*Like David*

David understood that vengeance was God's responsibility, not his. And when God finally exacted justice for Saul's rebellion, David refused to delight in the king's death. Read Psalm 82:3 in the margin. David uses four words to describe types of people.

"Defend the cause of the weak and fatherless; maintain the rights of the poor and oppressed."
Psalm 82:3

&&&

Which of these four words describes King Saul?

❑ weak ❑ fatherless ❑ poor ❑ oppressed

Think of a person who has harmed you. How would your feelings toward this person change if you think of him or her in this way? In the margin explain your answer:

Here's the distinction between *vengeance* and *justice*:

• *Vengeance* is our desire for retribution against our offender.
• *Vengeance* is striving to settle the debt ourselves.
• *Vengeance* leads to bitterness.

God says that I am to surrender my desire for *vengeance*.
• *Justice* is the payment another demands from our offender.

• *Justice* is allowing someone else to settle the score.
• *Justice* leads to healing.

I can forgive, but I can never surrender another person's responsibility to seek justice. So many of us struggle with the question: If God has really forgiven me, why does He make me suffer the consequences of my sinful actions? God instituted consequences for at least three reasons.

1. Consequences promote order in society. Imagine the chaos if everyone did as they pleased without any consequences. If your boss ticks you off, kill him. If you're running a little short of cash this month, steal some. If the attorney's questions are too personal, lie. If your neighbor's wife excites you, sleep with her. The whole rationale for the establishment of government was to provide a means to enforce God's code of conduct and save the world from anarchy.

God uses consequences to maintain order in our families, our churches, and our society. The father who prematurely posts bond for his son accused of drunk driving, the church leader who covers over the sin of a church member, and the victim who argues leniency in the sentencing of his offender all may have wonderful motives. But they are tampering with God's method for maintaining order.

2. Consequences serve as a deterrent to others. That is why Paul instructed the young pastor Timothy not to cover over the sins of church leaders: "Those who sin are to be rebuked publicly, so that the others may take warning" (1 Tim. 5:20). I believe this command relates to other arenas of life as well as to the church. Although your teenage daughter may truly repent after her third speeding ticket, revoking her driving privileges might deter not only her but also another teenager from engaging in reckless behavior. Terminating an employee for padding his expense account may promote a sudden surge of honesty among other employees as well. Negative consequences can be a deterrent to evil.

3. Consequences inoculate us against further disobedience. I once counseled a man who had been involved in an emotional affair for several years but had finally broken it off. God used many events to get his attention during his years of disobedience, including the loss of his business. Although the affair was over, Jack was still suffering the effects of a failed business and broken trust with his wife. "If God has truly forgiven me," he asked, "why do I keep suffering the consequences of my sin?" I suggested that he view these consequences in a different light, asking, "How likely are you to get involved with another woman?" He said: "Every time I see another woman I want to run in the opposite direction. I never want to go through that pain again."

Walking the Tightrope

Admittedly, sometimes a thin line separates *vengeance* and *justice*. I may think I'm seeking justice when, in fact, I'm thirsting for vengeance. That's why it's best, whenever possible, to allow someone else to mete out the consequences for injuries we suffer. If we're wronged by another person, Christ says our response is to "forgive from the heart." If there must be consequences, if at all possible, let someone else demand them. Specifically, the Bible teaches three administrators of justice in society.

1. The government administers justice. Among other passages in Scripture, Jesus' story in Luke 18:1-8 and Paul's teaching in Romans 13:1-4 clearly illustrate and teach that the government is to enforce justice. The wife who is physically abused, the adult who is concerned about a child's welfare, or the citizen concerned about a neighbor's illegal activity never need to be reluctant to appeal to the government for help. Although we can personally forgive the offender if we have suffered loss, we can appeal to the government for justice.

2. The church has a role in delivering justice. Many times the offenses we suffer have consequences that impact the body of Christ. A church member who has bilked you out of your life savings has certainly damaged you, but his dishonesty could also harm other Christians and the reputation of Christ. You might be able to forgive him personally; you're probably not the best person to confront him about his poor Christian testimony. Someone needs to, and Jesus has given Christians a very precise procedure to follow in that situation (see Matt. 18:15-20). We'll discuss this procedure to restoration in the next unit.

3. God is the ultimate arbiter of justice. Occasionally when we have been wronged, God will directly intervene by bringing disastrous judgments against our offender—judgments like illness, financial reversal, family disruptions, or even death. Numbers 16:31-32 tells that as a result of Korah's relentless attacks upon Moses, God opened up the earth and swallowed Korah and his followers. Moses did not control this dire solution; God alone took care of the problem.

A Closing Thought

Chuck Swindoll clearly distinguishes between forgiveness and consequences in his book on the life of David:

Grace means that God, in forgiving you, does not kill you.

Grace means that God, in forgiving you, gives you the strength to endure the consequences. Grace frees us so that we can obey our Lord. It does not mean sin's consequences are automatically removed. If I sin and in the process of sinning break my arm, when I find forgiveness from sin, I still have to deal with a broken bone.[2]

⁂

Place a check beside the paragraph below that more nearly describes you right now:

____ If you're struggling to move past deep wounds inflicted by another person, I encourage you to release your desire for vengeance and allow God or others to pursue justice. Trust me, He can settle the score much more effectively than you!

____ If you desire forgiveness from God or others, do not become discouraged over the lingering consequences of your sin, but view those consequences as a gift designed to keep you close to the Father who loves you.

---

[1] Max Lucado, *In the Grip of Grace* (Dallas: Word, 1996), 116-7.
[2] Charles R. Swindoll, *David* (Dallas: Word, 1997), 211.

Unit Four

Forgiveness, Forgetfulness, and Reconciliation

In a popular television program called Queen for a Day some unsuspecting home-maker was adorned with a crown and scepter, and treated royally for half an hour. I want to invite you to participate in a similar game we'll call "Pastor for a Day." You have been selected suddenly from your congregation to sit in your minister's chair. Instead of a crown and scepter, we're going to give you a Bible, plus three people who have come to you for counsel. What advice will you offer in each of their situations?

Sally tells you that during their eight years of marriage her husband John has physically abused her. Recently Sally persuaded John to attend a marriage seminar offered by her church. John was impressed with what he heard, and when the speaker invited those in the audience who wanted to become Christians to raise their hands, Sally was thrilled to see her husband respond. However, within several days the physical abuse resumed, as evidenced by the bruises you notice on her arm.

"That night after the seminar," Sally says, "John asked me to forgive him, and I did. But now things are worse than ever, and I'm really afraid. I've asked several friends if they thought I should move out, and they said: 'No, if you move out you're giving him a reason to divorce you. If you've really forgiven him, you'll try to keep your marriage together. Trust God to take care of you.'

"What do you think, Pastor?" Sally asks. "Should I stay, or leave?"

So I ask you, Pastor for a Day, does forgiveness demand that Sally remain with her husband? Why or why not?

Frank, a church leader, has invited you to lunch to discuss a matter that has been troubling him. You dread such appointments because they so often result in a request for you to don your black-and-white referee outfit and make a call that's likely to be criticized either way you go.

Frank begins: "Pastor, as you know, you requested that Bill and I serve on a committee. However, I don't believe we'll be able to work together. I haven't told this to anyone, but 10 years ago Bill and my son were involved in a business deal, and Bill cheated my son out of $25,000.

Although he never admitted his wrong, our family forgave him and refused to press charges. But I have to tell you, Pastor, I don't trust him and would feel like a hypocrite serving with him. So you need to decide which one of us you want to serve on the committee."

Pastor for a Day, is Frank's concern legitimate, or is he still harboring bitterness toward Bill? Explain your answer—and try to enjoy your lunch!

Sara is one of your most faithful church members, as is her husband, Steve. Several years ago, Sara tells you, her father began an affair with his secretary, and to everyone's shock, divorced his wife and married his lover. Since then her father and his new wife have lived in a different state and have had no contact with Sara, Steve, and their young daughter. But last week Sara received the following letter:

Dear Sara:

I know you cannot understand what happened between your mother and me; our problems were not her fault alone. My choice to divorce her and marry Denise may not have been the best choice, but it was the only alternative I thought I had for any measure of happiness for the rest of my life.

Denise and I are moving back and want to build a relationship with you, Steve, and little Darla. I am not asking you to condone my choices, but please do not deny me the pleasure of seeing my only grandchild. You have said that you forgave me for my mistakes and yet have resisted all attempts at reconciliation. How can you truly forgive me and yet refuse to have any contact with me? I am really in no position to demand anything from you, but I am asking you to search your heart and ask God whether or not you have, in fact, forgiven me. If you have, I believe you will allow me to see my granddaughter.

I await your reply,

Dad

Sara tells you she doesn't believe her father has genuinely repented of his wrongdoing, and she's concerned about exposing her daughter to an adulterous grandfather who is "living in sin."

Pastor for a Day, is Sara's demand for repentance really a thinly veiled desire for vengeance? ❏ Yes ❏ No

If she has released her father of his obligation to her, shouldn't she desire some reconciliation with him? ❏ Yes ❏ No

How long must her father continue to pay for his mistakes?

We've identified some misunderstandings about forgiveness that prevent people from either granting or receiving this all-important gift. Some people are confused about forgiveness and repentance, thinking that their offenders must demonstrate remorse for their actions before forgiveness is granted. Others are hesitant to forgive because they believe forgiveness means releasing their offenders of any consequences.

The three counseling situations described illustrate a third barrier to forgiveness: confusing forgiveness with reconciliation. Maybe you're hesitant to offer forgiveness because you have absolutely no desire to be reunited with a mate who has cheated on you, a friend who has slandered you, or your boss who demeans you.

We'll explore the difference between forgiveness and reconciliation. While I can unilaterally forgive another person, I cannot unilaterally be reconciled to my offender. Forgiveness depends upon me; reconciliation depends upon us.

Forgiveness depends upon me; reconciliation depends upon us.

The Case for Reconciliation

While extolling the virtue of forgiveness, some people downplay the importance of reconciliation. They say it's vital that you forgive your adulterous mate or incestuous relative, but whether or not you ever re-establish a relationship with that person is of secondary importance. Such an attitude toward reconciliation contradicts the teaching of Scripture.

⚶

Read the following Scriptures that discuss the importance of unity among Christians and record in the appropriate column the reasons for or the benefits of unity:

	Reasons for Unity	Benefits of Unity
Psalm 133:1:	_____	_____
Matthew 5:23-24:	_____	_____
Ephesians 4:3-4:	_____	_____

Make no mistake about it: God desires reconciliation among Christians for at least two important reasons. First, reconciliation testifies to God's power. The corollary to that is that disharmony among believers is a detriment to our witness. Without reconciliation, we fail to offer the world what Jesus pointed to as the signal evidence of our faith–our ability to live in harmony with other Christians. "By this all men will know that you are my disciples, if you love one another" (John 13:35).

The second reason God desires our reconciliation is that it empowers us to resist the attacks of the enemy. One of Satan's primary strategies is to divide, isolate, and conquer his victims. Two Christians become involved in a dispute over a failed marriage, an unsuccessful business venture, or a betrayal in a friendship. One or both parties becomes disillusioned and falls away from the church into spiritual isolation. Once cut off from the spiritual nourishment and encouragement of a body of believers, they become easy marks for the enemy's final assault.

Reconciliation is important among Christians because there is spiritual strength in numbers. We should never forget that we are in a war—a spiritual war—"against the spiritual forces of evil in the heavenly realms" (Eph. 6:12). That's why it is vital that we put aside our differences and join forces to battle against our common enemy instead of against one another. Nevertheless, while reconciliation between Christians is always preferable, it isn't always possible. The apostle Paul advised: "If it is possible, as far as it depends on you, live at peace with everyone" (Rom. 12:18).

Although I can immediately, unconditionally, and continually forgive someone who has hurt me, I may not always be able to effect a reconciliation with my offender. Similarly, if I have hurt another person, I can

Without reconciliation, we fail to offer the world what Jesus pointed to as the signal evidence of our faith—our ability to live in harmony with other Christians.

express my desire for reconciliation, but I am in no position to demand it, just as I can ask for his forgiveness, yet not demand it. The offended person, not the offender, holds all the cards.

Husbands are particularly notorious for not understanding this important principle. Josh had been verbally abusing his wife for years. After one particularly violent argument, Alice finally demanded that he move out of the house, which he did. Josh now recognizes how wrong he has been and has sought help from a Christian counselor. He cannot understand, however, why Alice will not let him move back into their home. The more he demands to return home, the more resistant Alice becomes. The more resistant she becomes, the harsher Josh becomes, and the relationship spirals downward.

Three Necessary Ingredients

I explained to Josh the three ingredients necessary to effect a reconciliation with someone we have wronged—repentance, restitution, and rehabilitation. Some, if not all, of these three ingredients may be required before the person we've wronged will choose to resume or rebuild the fractured relationship, even after that person has fully forgiven us.

1. Repentance

While I can forgive a person who never admits that he has hurt me, I probably can never be reconciled with him. Why? Relationships are built on common ground. The prophet Amos asked the question, "Can two walk together, except they be agreed?" (Amos 3:3, KJV).

Obviously, it's possible to maintain relationships with people who disagree with us on some issues. You may like Mexican food while your mate prefers Italian. Usually a person's political affiliation is not a litmus test for a friendship. In many churches, premillenarians and amillenarians co-exist peacefully, along with the majority who have no idea what those words mean. Yet, on important issues, there must be common agreement for a relationship to thrive, and there's no more important issue (at least in most folks' minds) than how another person treats us. If we feel we've been severely wronged, and the other party maintains his innocence, then there's a rupture in the relationship.

That truth applies also to our relationship with God. Failure to acknowledge our sin, even as Christians, breaks our relationship with

**Confession of our sin
is necessary to maintain
our relationship with God.**

*"If we claim to be without sin, we
deceive ourselves and the truth is not
in us. If we confess our sins, he is
faithful and just and will forgive
us our sins and purify us from all
unrighteousness. If we claim we
have not sinned, we make him
out to be a liar and his word
has no place in our lives."*
1 John 1:8-10

our Heavenly Father. In fact, it's that very relationship Amos had in mind when he wrote, "Can two walk together, except they be agreed?" The prophet was asking the Israelites a rhetorical question: How can you expect God's blessings when you won't admit your sin? Confession of our sin is necessary to maintain our relationship with God.

Admittedly, this is a controversial issue in many circles. Some Christian teachers maintain that confession of sin for a Christian is redundant and unnecessary. "If Jesus Christ forgave you of all your sins when you trusted in Him, why do you need to ask forgiveness again?"

Good question, but one that fails to differentiate between judicial and parental forgiveness. When we place our faith in Jesus Christ for our salvation, we're declared "not guilty" by God the Father. Judicially (legally), God has forgiven us. We are His children, and nothing we do will ever change that relationship.

Forgiveness does not exempt us from experiencing God's parental disapproval for our sin. For example, when one of my daughters disobeys me, I don't disinherit her and throw her out of the house to fend for herself. She will always be my child, regardless of her behavior. However, there will be a disruption in our relationship as long as she is unwilling to admit her wrong. I choose to discipline her, and for a period of time that discipline may drive her away from me. Only when she's willing to admit her mistake and ask my forgiveness will there be a reconciliation in our relationship.

The apostle John had that parental type of forgiveness in mind when he penned the words in the margin. John is saying to believers—not unbelievers—that as long as a Christian refuses to admit his sin, he is calling God a liar. Can you see how such an accusation might result in God's disapproval and discipline? Confession—agreeing with God about our sin—is necessary for reconciliation with Him.

Pause and pray about your relationship with God. Confess any sins you've hesitated to or been unwilling to confess. How does your confession change your relationship with God?

_____

How does it change you?

_____

The same truth applies in our relationship with other people. We must be willing to admit our mistakes and acknowledge the pain we have caused another person before we can ever hope for reconciliation.

ₒₒₒ

Pause and pray again. Are you ready, with God's help, to admit to another person a hurt you've caused them? ❏ **Yes** ❏ **No**

How can confession change your relationship with the person?

_____

How does it change you?

_____

2. Restitution

Before I choose to rebuild a broken relationship with someone who has wronged me, I may want to see an offer of some restitution or payment for the offense. Obviously we need to be careful here not to confuse restitution with revenge. Revenge is the desire to see my offender suffer for the pain he has inflicted on me. As we saw in unit three, revenge is usually futile because it can never adequately compensate us for the hurt we have suffered. The parent whose child is murdered may desire to see the killer suffer a slow, painful death, but that will never bring his child back to life. Revenge is best left in the hands of God.

However, restitution is our attempt to demonstrate genuine repentance to someone we have wronged. While revenge is the payment we demand from our offender, restitution is the payment we volunteer to another person we have offended.

ₒₒₒ

In the margin list as many synonyms or synonymous phrases for *revenge* and *restitution* as you can muster. I've provided an example of each to get you started.

The familiar story of Jesus and Zacchaeus illustrates the relationship between genuine repentance and restitution. The tax collector was despised by the Jews. In Jesus' day, tax collectors were notoriously dishonest. They were authorized by the Romans to assess taxes, but they

Revenge: punishment

_____

_____

_____

Restitution: paying a debt

_____

_____

_____

were free to inflate the amounts due and pocket the difference. Imagine having an IRS agent demand $10,000 from you and learning that he sent only $2,000 to Washington, D.C., using the rest to buy a new fishing boat. Such practices were legal in the Roman Empire and explain why the Israelites lumped tax collectors together with sinners and Gentiles.

In spite of his great wealth, Zacchaeus was spiritually bankrupt. Fortunately he recognized it, so when he heard that Jesus was coming to Jericho, he was willing to do whatever was necessary to catch a glimpse of the Savior. You can read their poignant encounter in Luke 19:3-6. Luke did not tell us all that went on in Zacchaeus' home that day, but apparently Zacchaeus embraced Jesus' message as evidenced by the response appearing in the margin.

Obviously, Zacchaeus' gift to the poor could never atone for his sin against God. Likewise, his willingness to compensate his victims four-fold was generous, but it was incapable of erasing the simple fact that he had wronged them. Nevertheless, Zacchaeus' restitution was evidence of the sincerity of his repentance and desire for reconciliation both with God and his neighbors.

Imagine for a moment that you were one of Zacchaeus' victims. He has extorted $10,000 from you through an inflated tax bill. Because of his dishonesty, your children will have to forfeit going to college next year. Yet as a follower of Christ, you have forgiven Zacchaeus of his sin. You have no desire for revenge, but neither do you have any desire for a relationship with this guy. As far as you are concerned, he's history.

One day your best friend says: "Did you hear the news? Zacchaeus has become a Christian. I was thinking, I'm sure he could use some Christian friends at this point in his life. Why don't we invite him to be a part of our supper club?" Although you're genuinely glad to hear of Zacchaeus' conversion, you have no desire to associate with this cheat. You're trying to think of a graceful way to blackball your friend's suggestion, when he adds, "And, by the way, did you hear that Zacchaeus is going to pay anyone he has cheated four times the amount of money he owes them?" Your attitude would likely change at that moment. Why? Because restitution validates the sincerity of repentance.

"But Zacchaeus stood up and said to the Lord, 'Look, Lord! Here and now I give half of my possessions to the poor, and if I have cheated anybody out of anything, I will pay back four times the amount.' Jesus said to him, 'Today salvation has come to this house.'"
Luke 19:8-9

Pray about an offense you have committed against another. What restitution might you offer to validate your repentance?

3. Rehabilitation

Another requirement for reconciliation is the rehabilitation of our offender. Before we choose to reestablish a relationship with someone who has wronged us, we may want some assurance that our offender has truly changed so that we aren't victimized again. The Bible teaches that genuine repentance is evidenced by a change in behavior.

Many people confuse repentance with sorrow. I've counseled abused wives who considered returning to their mates because their husbands were so grief-stricken over the separation. I usually question the sincerity of the husband's remorse. "Do you think it's possible that your husband is upset mainly because he no longer has someone to cook his meals, wash his clothes, or sleep in his bed?"

We can be sorry for the consequences of our sin without ever repenting. But godly sorrow leads to definite change in our life. The word *repent* comes from the Greek word *metanoeo* meaning "to change one's mind." Repentance is a change of mind that leads to a change of direction. Picture a person who realizes he is headed in the wrong direction, executes a U-turn, and heads in a new direction. That's repentance.

Before we rebuild a relationship, we'll probably want some evidence that our offender not only is sorry for actions, but has made some definite changes in behavior.

"Godly sorrow brings repentance that leads to salvation and leaves no regret, but worldly sorrow brings death."
2 Corinthians 7:10

Pray a third time about the offense you've recalled, specifically about yourself as the offender. What would demonstrate a changed direction to the person you've offended?

_____

Do you suppose they would answer the prior question in the same way as you? ❏ Yes ❏ No

The kind of rehabilitation necessary for reconciliation doesn't happen instantaneously, and it rarely takes place in a vacuum. Healing a broken relationship takes time, and it usually requires the spiritual assistance of other people. Paul taught about restoration in the verse in the margin.

The word translated *restore* is a Greek word used for setting a broken bone. For a bone to properly heal it needs to be placed in a protective cast and given time to properly mend. In the same way, when a person engages in behavior that destroys trust in a relationship, he or she needs

"Brothers, if someone is caught in a sin, you who are spiritual should restore him gently. But watch yourself, or you also may be tempted."
Galatians 6:1

to be surrounded by the spiritual help of other Christians and needs time to heal properly. A marriage fractured through a few moments of adulterous pleasure may take years to rebuild. That's why offenders are wrong to demand immediate reconciliation, and why the offended are unwise to offer it. Proper healing in a relationship takes time.

Forgiving and Forgetting

In the remainder of this unit, we need to explore the relationship between forgiving and forgetting. While forgetting an offense may be a result of forgiveness, it is neither the means nor the test of genuine forgiveness. Many people confuse forgiving with forgetting, resulting in two equally disastrous consequences.

First, equating forgiving with forgetting can short-circuit the forgiveness process. Attempting to forget our sins or the sins of others against us may provide temporary relief, but not lasting healing. Offenses require the surgical procedure of forgiveness, or else they'll metastasize into bitterness.

A second negative outcome that can arise from confusing forgiving with forgetting is unnecessary guilt. It surfaces in questions like these: "If God has really forgiven me, why do I keep remembering the affair I had five years ago? Maybe I haven't genuinely repented of my sin." "If I've really forgiven my father, why can't I forget the hurtful words he spoke to me decades ago? Maybe I haven't really forgiven him."

"See to it that no one misses the grace of God and that no bitter root grows up to cause trouble and defile many."
Hebrews 12:15

You may have asked yourself these kind of questions. Fill in the blanks below with your own bewildered, wondering words:

- If God has really forgiven me, why do I keep remembering _____? Maybe I haven't genuinely repented of my sin."
- If I've really forgiven _____, why can't I forget _____? Maybe I haven't really forgiven him."

We're to forgive "just as in Christ God forgave you" (Eph. 4:32). Doesn't the Bible teach that when God forgives, He forgets? If God can bring Himself to forget our sins against Him, why should we find it so difficult to forget our petty injuries from others? I admit that I've used those clichés myself in some past sermons that hopefully will be forgotten! Let's examine this premise closely. When God forgives, does He actually forget our sins? The Bible seems to teach that He does.

֍֍

Read the passages in the margin, and underline words or phrases that seem to indicate God forgets our sins.

I admit that these verses might lead us to believe that God completely forgets our sins when He forgives us. But is it really possible for God to forget what His creatures have done? Does God have a case of heavenly Alzheimer's? Paul declared: "For we must all appear before the judgment seat of Christ, that each one may receive what is due him for the things done while in the body, whether good or bad" (2 Cor. 5:10).

If, after we become Christians, God simply forgets all of our sins—past, present, and future—then it stands to reason that at the judgment seat of Christ, only the good things we've done will come to light. But the verse above teaches that God will judge all our deeds to determine, not our eternal destiny, but our eternal rewards—rewards tied to our obedience or disobedience in this life.

Am I saying I don't believe the Bible when it says that "God forgets our sins?" Before you write me off as a heretic, allow me to offer another way of understanding these verses. Read the paragraph in the margin.

Bible writers used the familiar to explain the unfamiliar, much as a teacher might drop an apple to the ground to explain the law of gravity. The Scriptures that speak of God forgetting sin are attempts to express the completeness of God's judicial forgiveness. When we receive God's forgiveness, we no longer have to fear the eternal consequences of our sin. I like what one person said about God's forgiveness: "He casts our sin into the depths of the sea ... and then posts a sign that says 'No Fishing.'"

Christians never have to worry that one day God will dredge up our sins and say, "I know I forgave you, but the more I think about what you did, I can't allow you into heaven. Adios." No, God has eternally removed the eternal consequences of our sins.

Such forgiveness does not require God to forget our actions. Romans 4:7-8 (which quotes Psalm 32:1-2) has helped me understand God's forgiveness more completely: "Blessed are they whose transgressions are forgiven, whose sins are covered. Blessed is the man whose sin the Lord will never count against him."

"As far as the east is from the west, so far has he removed our transgressions from us."
Psalm 103:12

"For I will forgive their wickedness and will remember their sins no more."
Jeremiah 31:34

"You will again have compassion on us; you will tread our sins underfoot and hurl all our iniquities into the depths of the sea." Micah 7:19

Although every word in the Bible is God-breathed, not every word is to be taken literally. For example, the Bible refers to God's eyes (2 Chron. 16:9), His ears (1 Pet. 3:12), His hands (Ex. 24:11), His heart (Hos. 11:8), and His feet (Gen. 3:8). Theologians refer to those verses as "anthropomorphisms"— attempts to explain an infinite God to finite man. Yet we know that God is spirit and therefore possesses no physical body. Nevertheless, He does see our actions, hear our prayers, and feel our pain.

"Having canceled the written code, with its regulations, that was against us and that stood opposed to us; he took it away, nailing it to the cross."
Colossians 2:13-14

Did you catch that last phrase? "Whose sin the Lord will never count against him." Our sin creates an indebtedness to God. We owe God for the transgressions we have committed. But Christ's death paid our sin debt in a transaction that Paul explained in the Scripture in the margin.

When you become a Christian, God takes the debt you owe Him, nails it to the cross, and declares it "paid in full," forgiving a debt without forgetting a debt. God will always remember our sin that required the blood payment of His own Son. But when God recalls our sin, it does not mean that He reneges on His promise to forgive our sins. When Satan brings our sins to God's attention (and passages such as Zech. 3:1; Rev. 12:10 indicate that he does just that!), God doesn't claim He has "holy amnesia." He reminds our accuser of the death of His Son that secured our forgiveness. Perhaps that's what John had in mind when he wrote, "But if anybody does sin, we have one who speaks to the Father in our defense—Jesus Christ, the Righteous One" (1 John 2:1).

Call a Christian friend. Read the Scriptures mentioned in the above paragraph over the phone to each other (from different versions if possible). Talk together about what they mean to each of you.

I've counseled people who have struggled with this issue of forgetting their sins. One woman who'd had a prolonged affair tried every technique imaginable to erase the memory of those years from her mind. But without any warning, scenes from that illicit relationship would flash across her mind at the most inopportune times: in church, while she was reading her Bible, even in intimate moments with her husband. Her question to me was simple: "If my repentance is genuine and God's forgiveness is complete, why do I still remember those experiences?"

I explained to her one important difference between forgetting and forgiving. Forgetting is a function of the brain; forgiveness is a function of the spirit. In his book *"I Should Forgive, But...,"* Chuck Lynch explained the power of memories this way:

All memories are stored in the brain by electronic impulses and by chemical transference. Messages are sent simultaneously from nerve to nerve both electronically and chemically. Memory is not a spiritual function–it's a biological function. Our brain can store at least six hundred memories a second.

That would work out to about one-and-a-half trillion bits of information if we were to live seventy-five years. That is awesome when I consider that I don't even remember what I had for breakfast two days ago.[1]

So when we encourage someone to forget, we're asking them to do the impossible. In fact, struggling to forget a past event can have just the opposite effect. The more we try to forget, the more we remember. Here's the bottom line: Forgetting offenses is not possible—and neither is it profitable. Since God has wired our bodies to permanently record our experiences, there must be positive benefits to remembering our sins.

Consider the experience of the apostle Paul. Before his conversion he was a persecutor of Christians and a blasphemer of God. As much as he may have wanted to, Paul could never escape the daily reminders of his past. As he went from church to church, he looked into the faces of those whom he had persecuted and the relatives of those he may have killed. Forget his past? Impossible.

Read carefully Paul's description of remembering his sins (see (1 Tim. 1:12-16). When you finish, in the margin list Paul's mistakes and sins remembered from his pre-Christian past.

Explain in a way a 10-year-old could understand why Paul was thankful in the midst of all those memories.

_____

_____

Paul explained three specific benefits of remembering our sins:

1. Encourages gratitude. "I thank Christ Jesus our Lord" (v. 12), Paul wrote. More than 30 years had passed since his conversion, yet he remained overwhelmed by God's gracious act of forgiveness. Are you? One reason God allows us to remember our sin is so we might continually recall His undeserved grace. Do you?

2. Extinguishes pride. "Christ Jesus came into the world to save sinners—of whom I am the worst" (v. 15). On God's sin scale, pride ranks right at the top. One way God encourages humility is by allowing us to recall our mistakes. Will you?

"God opposes the proud but gives grace to the humble."
1 Peter 5:5

3. Exhibits grace. Paul continued, "For that very reason I was shown mercy so that in me, the worst of sinners, Christ Jesus might display His unlimited patience as an example for those who would believe on Him and receive eternal life" (v. 16). Paul understood that his past sins made him Exhibit A of God's ability to forgive. To those who struggled with the possibility of God's forgiveness, Paul said: "Look at me. If God can forgive me, He can forgive you." Nearly 2000 years later, the record of Paul's blasphemous and murderous acts still encourages those who struggle with the issue of grace. Does this record encourage you?

Which of the three benefits of remembering our sins is most meaningful to you as you've studied this material? Why?

_____

_____

The Offenses of Others

What about the wrongs others commit against us? Over the years I've suggested the following steps for dealing with the memories of other people's offenses. Pause a moment to remember an offense against you for which you have forgiven your offender; think of that hurtful incident as you read through these four steps.

1. Release them if possible. Some of the trivial hurts of life can be dismissed from our consciousness. Recently a church member apologized to me for a comment she had made several months ago after a service. I wanted to be gracious to her, but I honestly couldn't recall what she had said. For whatever reason, I had dismissed her comment instead of nurturing it into a full-grown offense. I'm not always that forgiving, I can assure you (or better yet, ask my wife). However, overlooking the trivial hurts of life benefits us as much as it benefits our offender. Remember Proverbs 19:11?

In the past, what has prevented you from releasing a hurt?

_____

"A man's wisdom gives him patience; it is his glory to overlook an offense."
Proverbs 19:11

What do you need to do now for that to happen?

_____

2. Recall your own failures. Admittedly, some memories of past wrongs cannot be easily dismissed. They require action. Years ago, I served a church where a leader was caught in an adulterous relationship but ultimately repented of his sin. Another church member said to me, "I forgive him, but every time I see him I can't help but think about what he did." I appreciated his honesty and offered this suggestion: "The next time you see him, think about one secret sin in your past that you hope no one ever discovers. Picture in your mind what it would be like to have that sin announced, or better yet, projected on a video screen to the entire congregation. Then thank God for His forgiveness."

Jesus sounded a sobering warning to those who engage in self-righteous condemnation of others without honestly evaluating their own lives. Read those familiar words in the margin.

"Do not judge, or you too will be judged. For in the same way you judge others, you will be judged, and with the measure you use, it will be measured to you. Why do you look at the speck of sawdust in your brother's eye and pay no attention to the plank in your own eye?"
Matthew 7:1-3

🔥

Describe any change in your feelings or attitude about the sin of another as you think about your own sins becoming public.

_____

3. Remember your past act of forgiveness. The best remedy for painful memories is not forgetting the offense, but remembering your decision to forgive. If you're going to remember a wrong, make sure you also remember how you dealt with that wrong.

In writing on this topic, Chuck Lynch recalled the old westerns on television in which the good guy always carried two guns, one on each hip. Whenever the hero was in a shootout, he would draw both guns simultaneously, with lightning speed. Imagine you encounter someone who has wronged you in the past. You're equipped with two guns. The left gun represents the memory of what that person did to you; the right gun represents your act of forgiveness. The key is to draw both guns simultaneously. You don't draw on the memory of the sin without also drawing your act of forgiveness.[2]

4. Realize that healing memories takes time. I like the story about the group of workers striking against their company because of low wages. They marched in front of the company gates carrying placards that read:

"Time Heals. Time and a Half Heals More!" Obviously, the passing of time in and of itself cannot heal the wound of a serious offense. But time can diminish the sting of past memories if we've properly forgiven another person.

Corrie Ten Boom compared remembrances of past hurts to the sounding of a church bell. Such a bell is rung by pulling on a rope, but after the sexton lets go of the rope, the bell keeps on swinging. The bell keeps ringing slower and slower until there's a final dong and it stops. The analogy applies to forgiveness. "When we forgive, we take our hand off the rope. But if we've been tugging at our grievances for a long time, we mustn't be surprised if the old angry thoughts keep coming for a while. They're just the ding-dongs of the old bell slowing down." [3]

The "dongs" that continue to sound in your mind from grievances long past may or may not completely stop, but they can diminish in frequency and intensity. How? By making sure you have let go of the rope through the act of forgiveness.

How long ago did the offense you've recalled occur in your life? Describe any changes in the sting of that offense since you chose to forgive your offender. Pause to thank God that each passing day removes more of the sting of the offense from your life and frees you from that long ago hurt.

Insure that you've learned these four steps for dealing with hurtful memories by matching the following fragments into complete sentences:

1. Release	a. your past act of forgiveness
2. Recall	b. them if possible
3. Remember	c. that healing memories takes time
4. Realize	d. your own failures

[1] Chuck Lynch, "*I Should Forgive, But…*" (Nashville: Word, 1998), 27.

[2] Ibid, 36.

[3] Robert Jeffress, *When Forgiveness Doesn't Make Sense* (Colorado Springs, CO: Waterbrook Press, 2000) 138-9.

PART THREE

"Forgive Us ... As We Forgive"

I've been counseling with a man who became involved in an affair with a married coworker. This illicit relationship cost him his marriage, his children, his job, and his reputation. He lamented: "I would give anything if I could rewind the last six months of my life and start over. But that's impossible."

Have you ever felt that way? Have you thought, *If only I could take back a word spoken in anger, say no to that unwise suggestion, say yes to a forfeited opportunity, or salvage a broken relationship?* Unfortunately, life comes with no rewind button; but God does offer us a powerful antidote to heal the regrets of past mistakes. It's called forgiveness—humbly receiving it and freely giving it. God's design helps us to be people who live facing the future, regardless of the "if only's" of the past.

Up to this point, we've discussed forgiveness in theory by defining forgiveness and exposing four myths that sometimes prevent us from experiencing it. These four myths are the primary topics of Part Two.

Review the four myths and record them here to remind you of what forgiveness is not and how it does not work in our lives.

1. _____

2. _____

3. _____

4. _____

You can't give away what you don't possess or what you haven't received. That's why before you can ever grant forgiveness to others, you must first receive forgiveness in your own life: from God and then from others. These are the tasks revealed in Part Three. Give your best time and sincerest heart to the next two weeks so that you finish well the journey begun four short weeks ago.

Unit Five

Receiving the Gift and Giving It Away

Guilt is one of the most debilitating of all human emotions. It wreaks destruction in our relationships with others and in our relationship with God. Certainly some of the guilt pangs we feel are illegitimate. I hesitate to use the term false guilt because this kind of guilt is very real, although it's often unnecessary. Even our Christian culture can push unreasonable expectations that, if not met, tend to overwhelm us with guilt, such as:

- Women should not work outside the home.
- We must pray at least an hour a day to have an effective prayer life.
- We should never go into debt.
- The only way to properly educate our children is by sending them to a Christian school (or better yet, home school them).

Illegitimate guilt isn't nearly the problem some would have you believe it is. As I mentioned earlier, the usual reason people feel guilty is that they are guilty. All of us have certain things in our lives for which we feel ashamed. A prominent playwright in London supposedly sent an anonymous note as a joke to 20 of London's leading citizens. The note read: "All has been found out. Leave town at once." All 20 citizens immediately left the city.

Unresolved guilt affects us both emotionally and spiritually. One psychiatrist estimated that 70 percent of people in mental wards could be released today if they knew how to find forgiveness.

Guilt breaks our relationship with God because it produces separation. As Isaiah the prophet said, "But your iniquities have separated you from your God" (Isa. 59:2). When we deviate from God's standard, we instinctively run from Him. That's why we must learn to deal with guilt constructively.

"Fight the good fight, holding on to faith and a good conscience. Some have rejected these and so have shipwrecked their faith."
1 Timothy 1:18-19

In the verses in the margin, Paul presented the basics of dealing constructively with guilt. Identify and write below the two essentials for a healthy Christian life:

1. _____

2. _____

Read the following questions and check your answer to each:

Are you suffering from a guilty conscience? ❑ Yes ❑ No
Do you wish you could erase certain scenes from your past?
❑ Yes ❑ No
Does unresolved guilt keep you from God? ❑ Yes ❑ No

If you answered yes to any of these questions, I have good news for you. Forgiveness from the past is possible. If you find that difficult to believe, then consider the experiences of King David, the most outstanding of Israel's kings. He became intoxicated by his own accomplishments, acting as if he were exempt from God's standards.

Read the story of David's downfall in 2 Samuel 11:1-5. In the margin identify his mistake that started the dominoes falling around him.

From one isolated act—not going out to battle with his troops as any dedicated king would do—David became another victim of God's universal law: "A man reaps what he sows" (Gal. 6:7). In this case, David's sowing resulted in Bathsheba's pregnancy. David panicked at this news. Petrified that someone would discover his sin, he orchestrated a masterful cover-up plan. Continue reading in 2 Samuel, verses 6-9.

On a scale of 1 to 10, rate the two men in the story on the following qualities:

	David	Uriah
Self-centeredness	_____	_____
Focus in life	_____	_____
Display of character	_____	_____

Uriah had more integrity than his king. He reasoned that if the men under his command could not enjoy sex with their wives, he should set a good example by restricting his own pleasure. (Don't you hate it when people under your authority show you up like that?)

David had to resort to Plan B. Read 2 Samuel 11:10-15,26-27. In the margin note your impressions of David's panic-driven plan.

David thought his secret was safe. Months elapsed while he experienced no consequences for his sin, so he made the mistake of confusing God's patience with tolerance. If you're living apart from God and haven't experienced any major calamity in your life, don't misread the situation. The only reason God has delayed His judgment is to give you an opportunity to repent.

A Christian leader I know was engaged in a compromising relationship. He was sure that no one knew about his clandestine meetings with a woman. That his behavior went undetected only emboldened him to more contact with her, but the leaders of his organization knew everything. In fact, they had set a date to confront and dismiss him if he did not acknowledge and repent of his misbehavior. Unfortunately he made the mistake of confusing patience with tolerance. He lost his position.

Solomon wisely observed: "When the sentence for a crime is not quickly carried out, the hearts of the people are filled with schemes to do wrong" (Eccl. 8:11). Just as the Christian leaders' board had set a date to confront him, so God had appointed a time to expose David. After six months, the prophet Nathan paid a visit to the king. He told of a wealthy man who had stolen the only possession of a poor man, a little ewe lamb, and had served it for dinner. When David heard the story of this great injustice in his own kingdom he cried out: "As surely as the Lord lives, the man who did this deserves to die! he must pay for that lamb four times over, because he did such a thing and had no pity" (2 Sam. 12:5-6).

Mark it down: "The more angry people become over the sins of others, the more guilty they usually are." After a dramatic pause, Nathan pointed his bony finger at David and said, "You are the man." In an instant, what had been done in secret became public knowledge. David had a choice to make. He could either continue to cover his tracks, or he could allow God to cover his sin. Exhausted from the unrelenting guilt of the past half year, David chose the latter. "Then David said to Nathan, 'I have sinned against the Lord.' Nathan replied, 'The Lord has taken away your sin. You are not going to die'" (12:13).

David wrote a beautiful psalm of confession about this moment in his life. Read the opening verses of Psalm 51 in the margin. Circle the actions David implored God to take in his behalf.

In addition to the requests you circled, David also pled to have his sin washed away and to be given "a pure heart" (51:10). David asked God to

"Have mercy on me, O God, according to your unfailing love; according to your great compassion blot out my transgressions. Wash away all my iniquity and cleanse me from my sin. For I know my transgressions, and my sin is always before me. Against you, you only, have I sinned, and done what is evil in your sight, so that you are proved right when you speak and justified when you judge."
Psalm 51:1-4

let him experience "joy and gladness," the renewal of "a steadfast spirit within me," and the restoration of "the joy of your salvation" (51:8,10,12).

David's words in Psalm 32 may reflect God's answer to his cries as he experienced the relief that accompanies forgiveness. Underline these verses in your Bible. Begin to memorize them.
- Are you tired of running from the past?   ❏ Yes ❏ No
- Would you like to experience the same relief that David felt when he received God's outrageous grace? ❏ Yes ❏ No

Fortunately David not only described his experience but also outlined for us some crucial steps for receiving God's forgiveness.

1. Honestly Evaluate Your Relationship with God

In Psalm 139:23-24 David was asking God to reveal any areas of sin or failure in his life. Pause now to pray the same kind of prayer; ask God to reveal to you where you have failed in each of these areas and relationships:

- God—unconfessed sin, unkept promises, failure to nurture a relationship with Him
- your parents or siblings—ingratitude or unresolved conflicts
- your spouse—harsh words, selfish attitudes, or ingratitude
- your children—failure to spend time with them or to provide spiritual leadership for them
- others—immoral relationships, people you have offended, friendships that need to be more Christ-centered
- habits—immoral or slothful habits displeasing to God
- possessions—trusting in money, dishonest business dealings, failure to be a good steward

What impressions did you receive from God in your prayer?

_____

How will you respond to His searching Spirit?   _____

_____

"Blessed is he whose transgressions are forgiven, whose sins are covered. blessed is the man whose sin the Lord does not count against him and in whose spirit is no deceit."
Psalm 32:1-2

"Search me, O God, and know my heart; Test me and know my anxious thoughts. see if there is any offensive way in me, and lead me in the way everlasting."
Psalm 139:23-24

For what are you most grateful concerning forgiveness?

_____

2. Acknowledge Your Failure to God

David made a curious comment in Psalm 51:4: "Against you, you only, have I sinned and done what is evil in your sight." The statement illustrates his understanding that all sin ultimately offends God. To experience forgiveness, first determine whom you have offended most. And at the top of your list should be "God."

When you acknowledge your failures to God, you're not telling Him something He doesn't already know. God doesn't slap His forehead and say: "You did that? I can't believe it!" God is not some ogre in heaven with a two-by-four, waiting to knock us out the moment we come admitting our guilt. Instead, He's like the prodigal's father, scanning the horizon for any sign of our coming home.

Picture the eyes of God looking for you, then finding you. Describe your feeling when you sense His gaze on you:

_____

Describe the look on His face and on yours: _____

_____

With the help of a concordance, choose a Scripture that confirms the truth about this possible encounter with God. Write it in the margin.

3. Receive God's Forgiveness

In W.H. Auden's poem "For the Time Being," King Herod said: "Every crook will argue: 'I like committing crimes. God likes forgiving them. Really the world is admirably arranged.'"[1] Cynical as this sounds, one part is true: God delights in offering forgiveness. Read again David's requests in Psalm 51 printed in the margin.

Circle the words used to describe God's character.

"Have mercy on me, O God, according to your unfailing love; according to your great compassion blot out my transgressions."
Psalm 51:1

God hates sin, but He loves to forgive sin. God doesn't offer forgiveness "While Quantities Last." Forgiveness is always available to those who ask for it. Read 1 John 1:9 in the margin. Underline the words John uses to describe God's character.

John described forgiveness for the sins we commit after we become Christians, sins that cause a rupture in our familial relationship with our Father. How? Sin always produces guilt. And guilt always breaks our relationship with another person.

Last week my daughter Dorothy presented me with her first-grade report card. The left side showed all As. The right-hand side had a straight line of Ss for her satisfactory conduct. "Dad, those are the same thing as As," she was quick to point out. My mind wandered back to the time I received my first report card. I'll never forget the horror I felt seeing all of those Ss on the card. I knew that A was the best you could do, and the further you proceeded down the alphabet, the worse it got. If an F was enough to fail you, then S must be enough to imprison you!

For three days I hid my report card from my parents. I remember feeling so uncomfortable with them, avoiding them whenever possible. Why? Because I felt guilty. Guilt broke our relationship, even though they weren't angry with me. If you're God's child, He may be displeased with your disobedience, but He isn't angry with you. He stands with outstretched hands ready to forgive if you will simply ask.

"If we confess our sins, he is faithful and just and will forgive us our sins and purify us from all unrighteousness."
1 John 1:9

Think creatively a moment, then complete the following phrase: Accepting God's eternal salvation but neglecting to ask for His daily forgiveness is like ...

_____

4. Refuse to Allow Satan to Paralyze You with Guilt

Once you have received forgiveness, Satan will continue to accuse you, as if he had grabbed you by the nape of the neck and said: "Where do you think you're going? Don't you remember what you've done? Why do you think God can use you?"

Whenever those guilt feelings come back, remember the extent of God's forgiveness. Although God doesn't forget our sin, He covers over it completely, as David prayed: "Hide your face from my sins and blot out all my iniquity" (Ps. 51:9).

"When you were dead in your sins and in the uncircumcision of your sinful nature, God made you alive with Christ. He forgave us all our sins, having canceled the written code, with its regulations, that was against us and that stood opposed to us; he took it away, nailing it to the cross."
Colossians 2:13-14

The apostle Paul used another analogy for God's complete forgiveness. In his day, prisoners incarcerated for a crime had a certificate placed over their cell listing their offenses, a "certificate of debt." Paul had that certificate of debt in mind when he wrote the verses in the margin:

Our debt certificate has been nailed to the cross! Based on Colossians 2:13-14, list the actions Jesus took to cancel your debt:

_____

_____

Our obligation has now become Christ's obligation, and He willingly assumed it. That's why Jesus cried out on the cross, "It is finished" (John 19:30), meaning literally "paid in full." The death of Christ accomplished what nothing else could—the complete and final payment for our sins.

Close your eyes for just a moment and quietly hum "Amazing Grace." Sing the words in your head and your heart, imagining that they are drifting heavenward in grateful confession to the God who forgives even "a wretch like me." Take as long as you need to meditate on the forgiveness of God, given in love to you, and allow yourself to be overwhelmed with praise and gratitude to God.

Now, about receiving forgiveness from others, I have some good news and some bad news. Ready? The good news is that God forgives us instantly and completely whenever we ask. The bad news? People aren't like God!

Receiving forgiveness from others can be difficult. Some would use David's statement, "Against Thee only have I sinned," as an excuse not to be overly concerned about seeking other people's forgiveness. But as we saw earlier, God desires that Christians enjoy unity with one another. Guilt severs that unity; forgiveness can restore it.

Paul declared that his goal in life was "to keep my conscience clear before God and man" (Acts 24:16). Whenever you wrong someone, that person holds an "account receivable" in his hands. He can choose to hold on to it, or he can release you from your obligation. It's his choice. While we can't control what another person does, we always have a responsibility to seek reconciliation. Let's look at four practical steps for seeking forgiveness from others.

1. Determine If You Need to Ask Forgiveness

For years Trevor had lustful thoughts about his best friend's wife, Barbara. After attending a spiritual life conference, Trevor determined to deal with his lust once and for all. He confessed his sin to Rick and Barbara. He could tell by their reactions they were stunned and embarrassed by his revelation.

Trevor was surprised when Rick and Barbara refused an invitation to dinner. In fact, they continued to refuse all invitations. Finally, Rick told him, "Trevor, Barbara is uncomfortable around you, and we think it would be best if we didn't see one another for a while." Trevor was both shocked and hurt. He had been sincere and transparent with them. Why couldn't they find it in their hearts to forgive him?

Trevor had broken one of the cardinal rules of forgiveness—seek forgiveness only from those you have wronged. While Trevor's lustful thoughts were certainly a sin against God that needed to be confessed to Him, they represented no real offense against Barbara—not yet, anyway.

Jesus taught that we should seek reconciliation only with those we've injured: "If you are offering your gift at the altar and there remember that your brother has something against you, leave your gift there in front of the altar. First go and be reconciled to your brother; then come and offer your gift" (Matt. 5:23-24). Many people misread and misapply these verses. Notice Jesus is not addressing the offended, but the offenders. He describes a worshiper who suddenly remembers someone he has wronged. The person with whom we seek reconciliation is someone who "has something against you," a person who's aware of our offense.

I'm frequently asked: "Should I confess an adulterous relationship to my spouse if he or she is unaware of it?" There's no easy answer here. Some would argue that since guilt breaks a relationship, confession is necessary to restore unity in the marriage. Others would argue that confessing a hidden sin may do even more damage to the relationship. Let me suggest a checklist for determining whether or not to ask forgiveness from those who are unaware of your actions:

- Is restitution necessary? If you've stolen money or property, you have an obligation to return it.
- What are the chances your offense will be discovered? Hearing from someone else would be more hurtful than hearing it from you.
- Will your confession help or hurt the other party? This is the bottom-line issue. Our desire to "confess" can be very self-centered. Sacrificial love entails our willingness to bear our own burdens instead of asking someone else to share the load.

"Do not let any unwholesome talk come out of your mouths, but only what is helpful for building others up according to their needs, that it may benefit those who listen."
Ephesians 4:29

Before you confess a hidden offense such as adultery, ask yourself if your admission will build up or tear down the other person.

§§§

Recall a personal situation in which you've wronged someone, unbeknownst to the one you've wronged. Use the previous checklist to decide whether you should confess to the person.

2. Schedule an Appointment to Meet the Offended Person

When you need forgiveness, arrange a face-to-face meeting. Remember, your circle of confession should be no larger than your circle of offense. If you've offended one person, you need to confess your fault only to God and that person. As you arrange such a meeting, I suggest you say to the person: "I need to discuss something important with you. Could I meet you at [time] at [location]?" Understandably, that person may try to pry out of you the reason for the meeting. Instead of revealing that reason, simply say, "This is something so important that I'd rather talk with you in person."

If it's impossible to meet with the offended person, the telephone is the next best method. Its major drawback is its inability to communicate facial expressions and body language, because the offended person needs to be able to sense your sincerity and remorse. Likewise, you need to be able to gauge his or her response to your request for forgiveness.

The least preferred method of communication is a letter. As someone once said, "The reason for asking forgiveness is to erase the past, not document it!" Obviously, without the ability to hear the tone of our voices, see our facial responses, or ask follow-up questions, another person could easily misinterpret our written words on a page.

I encourage you to make any sacrifice necessary to meet as quickly as possible. A clear conscience is critical. Jesus commanded us to drop whatever we're doing, including worshipping God, to be reunited with an offended party: "First go and be reconciled to your brother; then come and offer your gift" (Matt. 5:24).

§§§

Thinking of a personal situation in which you need to seek forgiveness, determine some options for time and location to meet with the one you've offended. Record them in the margin; then rank them as the one most likely to work, next most likely to work, and so forth.

Remember, your circle of confession should be no larger than your circle of offense.

3. Ask for the Other Person's Forgiveness

Seeking forgiveness should never be confused with making apology. An apology is a unilateral (one-sided) response to an offense. Apologies can be filled with genuine remorse ("Words cannot express how terribly I feel for running over your cat"), or they may barely admit the possibility of wrongdoing ("I may have made mistakes in our marriage.").

Seeking forgiveness certainly includes an admission of guilt, but it involves much more than that. Requesting forgiveness is asking the person you've wronged to release you from your obligation. Remember the slave in Jesus' story? Did he nonchalantly say to the king, "I owe you some money; sorry." No, he desperately wanted release from his debt: "Be patient with me ... and I will pay back everything" (Matt. 18:26).

Consider these essential guidelines for asking for forgiveness:

- *Refuse to blame others.* The confession that begins, "We share the blame for this problem. I'm willing to accept my share if you will," is doomed from the beginning. Even if the other person is largely responsible for the conflict, concentrate only on your offense.

- *Identify the wrong you've committed.* Don't try to minimize your offense by confessing only minor transgressions. A person guilty of incest who says to the innocent party, "I'm sorry I haven't been the kind of [father, uncle, and so forth] I should have been," is not dealing with the real issue and will only compound the resentment. Remember, the other person is already aware of what you've done; now he or she wants to know that you are fully aware of it.

- *Acknowledge the hurt you've caused.* The other person wants to know that you understand the pain that he or she has suffered because of your actions. Try and relive your offense through that person's eyes. Recently a friend who had disappointed me said: "I can't imagine the grief and embarrassment this must have caused you. I'm sure my mistake has kept you awake at nights and distracted you from doing your job. Will you please forgive me?" Such insight will help the other person to forgive. It helped me.

- *Ask the other person to forgive you.* Forgiveness is a transaction in which the offended releases the offender. To end your discussion without asking for such a release harms both of you. He or she needs to forgive as much as you need to be forgiven. However, do not demand forgiveness or even infer he should forgive for his own benefit. Instead, you might use words such as this: "I realize that I've wronged you by _____. I'll do my best to see that I never do this again, though I realize there's nothing I can do to erase

An apology is a unilateral (one-sided) response to an offense.

Requesting forgiveness is asking the person you've wronged to do something: to release you from your obligation.

the deep pain I've caused you. What I did was wrong, and I can blame no one but myself. I'm coming to you today asking if you could find it in your heart to forgive me for what I've done."

𝄞

Take time now to write out your confession for the same personal situation you've been considering through these steps. As you write, check to see that you're not violating the first essential step in asking for forgiveness: Refuse to blame others.

(Identify the wrong you've committed): _____

(Acknowledge the hurt you've caused): _____

(Ask the other person to forgive you): _____

4. Be Prepared for a Negative Response

Not every attempt at reconciliation results in a warm embrace and a happy ending. The other person may respond ambivalently ("I don't know. I'll have to think about it.") or even negatively ("You think a simple apology can erase all the pain you've caused me? Forget it!").

The following reasons may explain a refusal to forgive:

- He doesn't sense that you're remorseful. Attaching blame to others, lack of identifying the real offense, insincere voice inflections, or failing to understand the hurt inflicted are just some of the ways you preempt remorse in your request for forgiveness.
- She feels guilty herself. Remember the guilt-blame seesaw? If she is partly to blame for the offense or feels guilt about something else, she may find it difficult to release you from your obligation. Why? It's much easier to handle her own guilt if she can balance it with blame toward you.
- He wants restitution. He may forgive you for stealing $100 from him, but only when he's sure you intend to return the money.
- She fears the offense will be repeated. Remember that genuine repentance involves willingness to turn away from unacceptable behavior. Before she releases you from your guilt, she'll want evidence that you have indeed made such a change.
- He confuses forgiveness with reconciliation. An abused wife may be reluctant to forgive her husband if she assumes that granting forgiveness means automatically giving him a key to the front door.

The wronged church may find it difficult to forgive a fallen minister if members confuse granting forgiveness with rehiring the leader. Remember the maxim, forgiveness is granted but reconciliation is earned.

As you've studied the previous five reasons for someone's refusal to forgive, have they helped to explain a situation from your life that was brought to mind? In the margin record any insights you've gained about ongoing difficult situations or strained relations.

Even if someone refuses to forgive you immediately, don't be discouraged. Sometimes the wounds we inflict on others are quite deep, and people may need time before they can grant forgiveness. Sometimes, the wounded person is never willing to forgive, which is tragic, since forgiveness is the only way to heal those deep wounds. Regardless, there is freedom in having a clear conscience, knowing that neither God nor any person can accuse you of never attempting to make right a wrong.

You may be thinking that asking for forgiveness is the hardest thing you'll ever do. For some of us, granting forgiveness is just as challenging. For all of us, however, it's just as necessary, and this is where we'll direct our thoughts for the remainder of this unit of study.

I believe many Christians carry a list of people whom they'd like to punish for the pain or hurt they've caused. Who is on your list? Be brave enough to record their names or initials here:

_____

_____

Deep down you want to see these people suffer. The Bible labels that desire as "vengeance," and vengeance harbored long enough eventually becomes bitterness. Sometimes bitterness erupts into the violent acts we read about in the newspaper—an angry husband murders his entire family, a student jilted by his girlfriend climbs a tower and shoots at passing students, a terminated employee returns to the office to gun down his former coworkers. More often bitterness grows like a cancer, slowly

> **Remember, forgiveness is granted but reconciliation is earned.**

destroying everything it touches. That's why the writer of Hebrews warned us to let no root of bitterness grow in our hearts (see Heb. 12:15).

If holding on to vengeance—our desire to see our offender suffer—is the root of bitterness, then doesn't it make sense that the antidote to bitterness is letting go of that desire? That's the essence of forgiveness. The word *forgive* means to release our desire for and right to vengeance.

No story in human history better illustrates the process of granting forgiveness than the story of Joseph and his brothers. Joseph was the favorite of Jacob's 12 sons. Joseph's brothers hated him and sold him into slavery where, through a long series of miraculous circumstances, God elevated Joseph from slavery to Pharaoh's right-hand man. Ultimately, God brought Joseph's brothers to Egypt to buy food—from Joseph.

Genesis 45:1-4 records the climactic confrontation between Joseph and his brothers. Read those verses and imagine you are one of these brothers who so badly mistreated and hated Joseph. What are you thinking at this moment ...

... about what Joseph's next words will be? _____

... about your future? _____

As the shock wore off, the brothers must have been thinking: *This is it! Surely Joseph will get even with us now!* With sweat pouring down their faces, they slowly approached their brother, certain that this was their end. Never in their wildest dreams could they have anticipated Joseph's remarkable response.

Read Joseph's words in Genesis 45:4-5,7-9. Still imagining yourself as one of the brothers, in the margin write a one-word description of your reaction to this amazing invitation.

Think for a moment what would have happened if Joseph had not forgiven his brothers. Imagine that when his brothers came requesting grain, Joseph had answered: "You want food? Funny you should mention that. Just today I was thinking about how much I wanted food when you left me for dead in that stinking pit." If Joseph had held a desire for vengeance and allowed his brothers to starve to death, the lasting consequences would have reverberated throughout eternity.

I believe that Joseph illustrated one of life's most important choices: the choice to forgive. His remarkable choices not only ensured the development of the nation of Israel, from whom Jesus Christ would come to save the world, but also serves today as an inspiration and illustration for how we're to forgive others.

Work carefully through the five steps that follow on forgiving others. Think of a personal situation in which you have been wronged and can offer forgiveness. In the margin, write your response to each of the steps.

1. True forgiveness admits that someone has wronged you. How often have you heard the advice: "Instead of concentrating on what other people have done to you, focus on the wrongs you have committed"? Such counsel sounds pious, but is actually lethal to the process of true forgiveness. You cannot forgive another person without first acknowledging that they've wronged you. Lewis Smedes writes: "We do not excuse the person we forgive; we blame the person we forgive."[2]

Joseph understood the importance of assigning blame to his brothers. In his confrontation with them he did not say: "Now, guys, I know you didn't mean to sell me into slavery. You were probably just having a bad day. Let's forget this ever happened." Joseph is painfully direct: "You meant evil against me." Joseph was saying, "You and you alone are to blame for the years of unjust suffering I endured." Joseph understood that we cannot forgive people we aren't willing to blame.

2. True forgiveness acknowledges that a debt exists. Wrongs produce indebtedness. Before either we or our offenders can appreciate the freedom of forgiveness, we must first understand the obligation that comes from our offense. Before you can properly forgive another person, you must accurately assess what he or she owes you. Be as severe as you think you need to be. Remember, offenses always create obligations. "Because of your affair, I should divorce you." "Because of your negligence, I should sue you." "Because of your actions, I should prosecute you."

3. True forgiveness releases our offender of his or her obligation. The word *forgive* means to release another person from obligation. In the same way, you need to formally release your offender of his obligation toward you. Whether or not you choose to voice your forgiveness to your offender, you can express it to God. Let me encourage you to pray something like this: "What _____ did to me was wrong. He should pay for what he did, but today I'm releasing him of his obligation to me. Not because he deserves it, or has even asked for my forgiveness, but because You, God, have released me from the debt I owe You."

5. True forgiveness waits for the right time to confront the offender. In Joseph's example, we see an extended period of time between the day Joseph first encountered his brothers in Egypt and the day he finally revealed himself to them. Joseph was full of wisdom as well as grace. He understood that only those who are truly repentant can receive forgiveness, so he waited for the right time to confront his offenders.

Joseph longed for more than just the personal freedom that comes with forgiveness. He wanted to be reconciled with his family. He had to determine if his brothers were truly repentant. Before you verbally offer forgiveness, make sure your offenders are ready to receive it. Does she demonstrate any remorse for what she has done? Is he willing to speak to me, or is he avoiding me? Does she demonstrate any evidence of change in her life?

Go back through the questions above, writing out answers to them regarding the person and situation you've been considering throughout this section.

While repentance isn't necessary for granting forgiveness, it is vital for receiving forgiveness. Augustine once said: "God gives where He finds empty hands. A man whose hands are full of parcels can't receive a gift." If you sense that your offender is open to reconciliation and you choose to verbalize your forgiveness, you may want to follow Joseph's example. Consider these additional suggestions as a three-point checklist to determine whether or not you've really forgiven your offender.

1. True forgiveness resists unnecessary embarrassment. Before Joseph revealed himself to his brothers, he had all of his Egyptian servants leave the room (see Gen. 45:1). Joseph sought to keep his brothers offenses as private as possible. Obviously there are times when offenses have to be reported to others. However, if you've truly forgiven another person, keep his or her sin as confidential as possible.

2. True forgiveness relieves people of unhealthy sorrow. If you've sincerely forgiven someone, you'll attempt to relieve him or her of unhealthy remorse. I know that isn't nearly as much fun as watching your offender buckle under a weight of guilt. Such a response is not forgiveness; it's vengeance. By contrast, Joseph chose to relieve his brothers of their unhealthy grief. He told them, "Do not be distressed and do not be angry with yourselves for selling me here, because it was to save lives that God sent me ahead of you" (Gen. 45:5).

3. True forgiveness continually releases our offender of his or her obligation. When Jacob died, Joseph's brothers again began to worry. Could Joseph's forgiving spirit simply have been a charade to appease their aged father? Joseph reassured them with the words in the margin.

While understanding God's sovereignty facilitated Joseph's forgiveness, it doesn't explain it completely. I think Joseph had a much more "selfish" reason for releasing his desire for vengeance. He was tired of the solitary confinement that comes from bitterness. Joseph desperately yearned for reconciliation with his family.

Remember how his pent-up emotions erupted when he finally revealed himself to his brothers? "He wept so loudly that the Egyptians heard him, and Pharaoh's household heard it" (Gen. 45:2). Such tears come only from those who are tired of rehearsing wrongs from the past and are ready to repair broken relationships. Forgiveness isn't a one-time action of the heart, but a continual choice of the will. As someone said, "Forgiveness is surrendering the right to hurt you for hurting me."

"But Joseph said to them, 'Don't be afraid. Am I in the place of God? You intended to harm me, but God intended it for good to accomplish what is now being done, the saving of many lives. So then, don't be afraid. I will provide for you and your children.' And he reassured them and spoke kindly to them." Genesis 50:19-21

&&&

Through your work in this unit, have you ...
        ... admitted that you've been hurt?   ❏ Yes ❏ No
        ... acknowledged the debt you are owed?   ❏ Yes ❏ No
        ... released your offender of his obligation, knowing that in
                the process you're also releasing yourself? ❏ Yes ❏ No

If you answered no to any of these questions, pause and consider why. Finish your study by writing a prayer to God, expressing your heart's cry over your struggle to complete the process of offering forgiveness. Consider calling a mature Christian friend, reading the prayer to him or her, and asking for feedback and encouragement.

---

[1] Philip Yancey, *What's So Amazing About Grace?* (Grand Rapids, MI: Zondervan Publishing House, 1997), 163.

[2] Lewis B. Smedes, *The Art of Forgiving* (Nashville: Moorings, 1996), 178.

Unit Six

Does God Need Our Forgiveness?

I've just talked with a woman who desperately needs to forgive someone—she's just not sure who. Six months ago she went to her doctor complaining of digestive disorders and sharp stomach pains. The doctor suggested simply that she cut back on her daily heart medication.

But now, after further examination, the doctor informed her that she has inoperable stomach cancer. "Under the most optimistic scenario, you probably have a year to live," he told her.

The woman and her husband were understandably distraught when they talked with me. The misdiagnosis six months ago was about to rob a man of his life partner, four children of their mother, and a woman of her life. I knew that this committed Christian couple wanted to avoid the trap of resentment at any cost. They were willing to forgive—if they could only determine who was to blame for this tragedy.

Was it the doctor who failed to perform the appropriate tests six months earlier? Themselves for not seeking a second opinion at that time? The insurance company that recommended the doctor through their HMO? The manufacturing company nearby that continually releases pollutants in their neighborhood air?

As we learned last week, blame is a prerequisite for forgiveness. But determining blame isn't always simple. Visualize for a moment some injustice you've suffered—not a slight offense, but some deep hurt from which you're still attempting to recover. Briefly describe that offense.

_____

_____

With that offense clearly in mind, imagine that you've walked into the complaint department of your local department store. You've suffered an injustice that you want settled, and you're willing to let go of the debt owed to you, if only you can figure out whom to forgive. In the complaint department, there are several customer service windows willing to help you choose who or what to blame.

Window Number 1: Other People

Other people make the easiest targets—the irresponsible doctor, the unfaithful mate, the insensitive pastor, or the disloyal friend—to be held directly responsible for our suffering. Linking our pain to a specific face may not make forgiveness easy, but at least it makes it possible.

In your situation, whose face is directly linked to your pain?

_____

How likely are you to forgive this person now? Explain.

_____

_____

Ron Mehl told of an eight-year-old boy taking a test. Nervous over the exam and concerned about completing it on time, the boy wet his pants. Sick with worry and embarrassment, he looked up and saw his teacher motioning for him to come to her desk. *What am I going to do?* he wondered. Seeing that the boy seemed frozen in his chair, the teacher started walking toward the boy. *Oh, no!* he thought, *she's going to discover my accident and everyone will laugh at me. This is going to be terrible!*

What the boy couldn't see was a classmate, a little girl, coming behind him carrying a large fishbowl. She suddenly lurched forward, dropped the fishbowl, and sent water and fish flying everywhere. The boy was suddenly covered in fish-tank water. *There really is a God in heaven! What a wonderful gift! What a wonderful girl!* he exulted to himself, but because "boys don't like girls," he sneered, "What's wrong with you, you clumsy clod? Why don't you watch where you're going?" The class laughed while the teacher took the boy to change into some dry clothes. At lunchtime, everyone shunned the girl. She was an outcast.

When the day was over, the boy noticed the girl walking by herself. Softly, he said: "I've been thinking about what happened today. That wasn't an accident, was it? You did that on purpose, didn't you?"

"Yes," she said. "I did do it on purpose. I knew what had happened to you. You see, I wet my pants once, too."[1]

The Bible says that we all stand guilty and humiliated before God. But out of a deep desire to spare us from the consequences of our sin,

It's because of His willingness to suffer shame for us that we should be willing to cover over the mistakes of others.

God spilled out His Son's blood for us so that our sins might be covered. It's because of His willingness to suffer shame for us that we should be willing to cover over the mistakes of others.

In your situation, who has stood up for you, advocated for you, or encouraged you? Christ's sacrifice on our behalf is the exact opposite of blaming someone else for our suffering. He had a right to blame us, but He sacrificed to cover our sin.

On a scale of 1-10, with 1 being very unsatisfying, how satisfying is it
- to find someone to blame for your hurt? _____
- to find someone who'll cover your hurt with his or her understanding and love? _____
- to cover someone else's hurt with your understanding and love? _____

What insights do you gain about yourself from your answer to these three questions?

_____

_____

Window Number 2: Ourselves

Sometimes we need look no further than the mirror to find the appropriate person to blame for our suffering. Many times the injuries we sustain are self-inflicted. We may be the primary cause of a failed career, a devastating divorce, or a life-threatening illness. Even so, we need to learn how to forgive ourselves.

The subject of forgiving ourselves is hotly debated among forgiveness experts. Some argue that forgiving ourselves is as impossible as solitaire Ping-Pong. Just as it's impossible to be on both sides of the net at the same time, it's impossible to be on the giving and receiving end of forgiveness simultaneously. We can forgive others, but not ourselves, they claim.

Perhaps that's technically true. As the scribes asked, "Who can forgive sins but God alone?" (Mark 2:7). Only those we injure can offer us absolution from our guilt. But consider a truck driver who falls asleep at the wheel and collides with an oncoming car, killing an entire family. He has certainly injured others, but hasn't he also done irreparable harm to himself? Although he may receive the forgiveness of the family's relatives and will certainly receive God's forgiveness if he asks, isn't it possible that he might still feel guilty? A thousand "if only's" might flood his mind: If only I'd refused to work overtime ... stopped for a cup of coffee ... pulled over for a nap ....

Identify below some of the "if only" questions you have asked yourself, particularly applying them to the task of forgiving yourself in the personal situation you've been recalling.

_____

_____

Sometimes the only way to forgive ourselves is by remembering our humanity. After we've sought forgiveness from God and those we've injured, we may still need to release ourselves by recognizing our limitations, just as God recognizes them: "For he knows how we are formed, he remembers that we are dust" (Ps. 103:14).

If God is willing to accept our frailties, why don't we? If you tend to be particularly hard on yourself, why do you suppose you do that? Explain your thoughts:

_____

_____

Window Number 3: Circumstances

Recently a tragic accident at an amusement park claimed the life of a young mother. A large floating inner tube carrying eight passengers capsized, trapping the passengers underneath the water. One passenger was killed and others were injured. After months of investigation, an engineering team concluded that there was no human error involved, just a list of isolated factors converging to cause the freakish mishap.

Jesus spoke of a similar incident in Luke 13:4, in which 18 people were killed when a tower fell on them. He then asked rhetorically if these 18 victims "were more guilty than all the others living in

Jerusalem?" Jesus was saying that bad things happen to bad people and to good people. Towers fall on the just and the unjust.

So whom do we blame, and then forgive, in these kinds of accidents? Who is responsible for ...

- the unexplained downturn in the economy that costs us our jobs?
- the electrical spark near the fuel tank that downs a jetliner?
- the maverick cell that grows into a life-threatening disease?

Such questions lead some people, especially Christians, to a favorite blame target.

Window Number 4: Satan

In a televised interview with a world-famous clergyman the interviewer asked why God would allow such things as the tragic school shootings of recent years to happen. The minister replied that God was not responsible; Satan was. The interviewer must have wondered, but didn't ask: "Couldn't God have stopped Satan if He wanted to?"

The Bible teaches that Satan is the "prince of this world" (John 12:31), the "god of this age" (2 Cor. 4:4), and the "ruler of the kingdom of the air" (Eph. 2:2). Nevertheless, he's not all-powerful. Satan is a created being with definite limitations. Satan is like a junkyard dog on a very long chain. His freedom to destroy is considerable, but not unlimited. That's why he cannot be held ultimately responsible for our pain.

Read the verses in the margin. Who is responsible for any influence Satan may have in your life? Who is to blame?

_____

"When tempted, no one should say, 'God is tempting me.' For God cannot be tempted by evil, nor does he tempt anyone; but each one is tempted when, by his own evil desire, he is dragged away and enticed."
James 1:13-14

My family has endured frustration, broken promises, and defective merchandise over a washing machine we purchased months ago. Finally, tired of the run-around I was getting, I sped to the store, determined to see someone to end my consumer suffering.

A salesperson recognized me immediately and tried to head me off at the pass. "Dr. Jeffress, I'm doing everything I can do to clear this up." I assured her that while I appreciated her efforts, I wanted to talk to the person in charge. She suggested I might speak with the head of the appliance department, but I had no interest in that either. The only person I wanted to see was the manager of the store. He was ultimately responsible for correcting the injustice I had suffered.

Reluctantly, the salesperson escorted me to the office area. While I waited in the foyer, she buzzed him on the phone. I heard her whisper into the receiver: "No, he's here in person and wants to talk to you. ... No, he said he will only talk with you."

The manager finally appeared and, after endlessly tapping on the computer, he admitted the store's error and credited my account. The lesson I learned: When you want something settled, you go to the top!

The same principle applies to forgiveness. Assigning blame only to other people, yourself, circumstances, or Satan can prevent you from completing the forgiveness transaction. After all, wasn't Job right when he told God, "I know that you can do anything and that no one can stop you" (Job 42:3, TLB).

God is ultimately sovereign over everything that happens in His creation. He is the undisputed ruler of the cosmos. Therefore, anything that comes into our lives must come through His hands. After all, if His claim is true that "I am the Lord, and there is no other" (Isa. 45:6), then He is absolutely and ultimately in charge.

The subject of forgiveness cannot be complete until we have stripped away all the intermediate layers and come to the place of forgiving God. I realize that the concept of "forgiving God" is offensive to some and borders on the blasphemous to others. To claim that God needs to be forgiven implies that:

(a) God has sinned against us.
(b) God owes us for what He has done to us.
(c) We have the power to release God of His obligation to us.

Study the following Bible verses to determine if those implications are scripturally possible. After reading each one, write in the margin the truth taught about God and whether or not He needs to be forgiven.

"You are good, and what you do is good." (Ps. 119:68).

"But who are you, O man, to talk back to God? Shall what is formed say to him who formed it, 'Why did you make me like this?' does not the potter have the right to make out of the same lump of clay some pottery for noble purposes and some for common use?" (Rom. 9:20-21).

"For we do not have a high priest who is unable to sympathize with our weaknesses, but we have one who has been tempted in every way, just as we are—yet was without sin." (Heb. 4:15).

As I read these verses, I can understand my editor's alarm over a chapter on forgiving God. Clearly, God is incapable of sinning against His creatures and, therefore, owes us nothing. Even if He did, we're in no position to "forgive" our Creator of anything.

So instead of "forgiving God," let's change to "blaming God." No, that doesn't work either, because blame implies guilt, and we've just seen that God is guilty of nothing.

Perhaps the best description of this unit's struggle is "holding God accountable." Until you're willing to allow God to assume responsibility for a handicapped child, an economic hardship, or an untimely death, you may never be able truly to find freedom and forgive others.

Does the idea of holding God accountable have any validity? Does it seem heretical? Consider carefully the remainder of this unit's material as you honestly face this possibility.

I believe God's plan for your life and mine includes suffering. God readily accepts responsibility for everything that occurs in His creation. Consider God's words to Moses: "Who gave man his mouth? who makes him deaf or mute? Who gives him sight or makes him blind? Is it not I, the Lord" (Ex. 4:11).

Some well-meaning Christians, trying to defend God's reputation, prematurely excuse Him from any responsibility for human suffering. They say things like: "God is just as grieved about your baby's deformity as you are. As much as He wanted to, God could not violate the natural laws of genetics that resulted in your baby's defect." The first statement is absolutely true. God shares our every grief and carries our sorrow (see Isa. 53:4). I don't buy the second part. God is not captive to natural laws. He is not handicapped and unable to act (see Isa. 59:1).

God has full responsibility for all human suffering, including the wrongs others commit against us. He is sovereign. He either chooses to cause events to happen, or He chooses to allow them to happen. Either way, He is in charge.

"Surely the arm of the LORD is not too short to save, nor his ear too dull to hear."
Isaiah 59:1

⸻

In your situation, has your suffering been (check all that apply):

___ physical   ___ mental
___ spiritual   ___ emotional
___ financial   ___ relational
___ vocational   ___ damaged reputation
___ loss of standing   ___ loss of rest/sleep
___ loss of direction   ___ loss of purpose

In what ways did your relationship with God help you bear these difficulties?

_____

_____

Read carefully in the margin Peter's words from his sermon at Pentecost, preached to those who just a few weeks earlier had crucified Christ.

Who was responsible for Christ's death? Godless men nailed him to the cross, but they were only instruments to accomplish God's purpose.

⸻

Now let me ask you a question: If God is willing to accept the blame for the horrific death of His own Son, won't His strong shoulders bear the weight of responsibility for the hurt you have endured? Take a moment to write your answer.

_____

_____

_____

The claim that "God loves you and has a wonderful plan for your life" is more than an effective opener for an evangelistic booklet. The Bible repeatedly affirms that God has planned every detail of our lives—

"This man was handed over to you by God's set purpose and foreknowledge; and you, with the help of wicked men, put him to death by nailing him to the cross." Acts 2:23

every joy and every heartache, every success and every failure, every triumph and every tragedy. All are part of His sovereign plan.

The Author of that plan is not a capricious deity who arbitrarily moves us around like pawns on a cosmic chessboard. Instead, God's plan for your life—all of it—is based on His love for you. Read the following verses and write beside them in the margin the evidence they give for God's love.

"In your unfailing love you will lead the people whom you have redeemed." (Ex. 15:13).

"Your eyes saw my unformed body.
All the days ordained for me
were written in your book
before one of them came to be." (Ps. 139:16).

"A man's steps are directed by the Lord,
How then can anyone understand his own way?" (Prov. 20:24).

And the verse many Christians know, love, and quote: "For I know the plans I have for you,' declares the Lord, 'plans to prosper you and not to harm you, plans to give you hope and a future.'" (Jer. 29:11).

So could a God who loves you include unjust suffering and indescribable pain in His plan for you? C. S. Lewis brilliantly exposed the real problem in reconciling God's sovereignty with God's love:

We want, in fact, not so much a Father in Heaven as a grandfather in heaven ... whose plan for the universe was simply that it might be truly said at the end of each day, "A good time was had by all." ... I should very much like to live in a universe which was governed on such lines. But since it is abundantly clear that I don't, and since I have reason to believe, nevertheless, that God is Love, I conclude that my conception of love needs correction. ... The problem of reconciling human suffering with the existence of a God who loves, is only insoluble so long as we attach a trivial meaning to the word "love."[2]

The Bible promises that "God works for the good of those who love him, who have been called according to his purpose" (Rom. 8:28). Unfortunately, some of us—to echo Lewis—attach a trivial meaning to the word *good*. If we translate that word as "happiness," "prosperity," or "freedom from adversity," we're doomed to disappointment. Paul identified the "good" that God's plan is designed to accomplish in the next verse: "For those God foreknew he also predestined to be conformed to the likeness of his Son, that he might be the firstborn among many brothers" (8:29). God has designed a unique plan for your life with one purpose in mind: to mold you into the likeness of His Son.

Suffering must have a role in this plan. Look again at Jesus' life: "Although he was a son, he learned obedience from what he suffered" (Heb. 5:8). How is it that Jesus Christ, the perfect Son of God, could learn anything—and obedience in particular? Wasn't He consistently perfect and obedient? Believe me, this is on my growing list of questions to ask when I land on the shores of heaven.

I do understand this: God's plan for Christ included intense suffering. And if God's plan for His own Son included injustice and intense pain, should I be surprised when God's plan for my life includes the same?

⸙⸙⸙

Do you remember Paul's prayer in Philippians 3:10? Read it several times. In light of all you've just considered on the meaning of suffering, what was Paul ardently seeking?

_____

Have you prayed the same prayer? ❑ Yes ❑ No If so, describe the experience.

_____

_____

"I want to know Christ and the power of his resurrection and the fellowship of sharing in his sufferings, becoming like him in his death."
Philippians 3:10

Occasionally God allows us to see the purpose of our suffering. Joseph was able to see the hand of God in his experience. Read carefully the paragraphs on the following page. You will recognize Joseph's speech to his brothers. Circle the words and phrases that refer to God's plan as you find them.

"And now, do not be distressed and do not be angry with yourselves for selling me here, because it was to save lives that God sent me ahead of you ... But God sent me ahead of you to preserve for you a remnant on earth and to save your lives by a great deliverance. So then, it was not you who sent me here, but God. He made me father to Pharaoh, lord of his entire household and ruler of of all Egypt. Now hurry back to my father and say to him, 'This is what your son Joseph says: God has made me lord of all Egypt. Come down to me; don't delay. ... You intended to harm me, but God intended it for good to accomplish what is now being done, the saving of many lives'" (Gen. 45:5,7-9; 50:20).

Forgiveness becomes easier when we look past our offender's motivations and see God's hand supernaturally working all things together for good. But at times we'll have difficulty seeing any good from the pain we suffer, like Job, a man who lost everything: his assets, his children, and finally his health. Job's initial response of faith was followed by a long period of doubt. Job had some serious questions he wanted answered, and for an agonizingly long time God was silent.

Finally the answer came, but not the answer Job was seeking. Not once did God ever answer the "Why, Lord?"of Job's suffering. Read Job 38:2-5,12-13; 40:2 to learn God's answer.

In the margin summarize God's message in 21st-century language that an unchurched friend could understand:

Not an easy task, is it? Frederic Buechner summarized God's monologue to Job this way:

God doesn't explain. He explodes. He asks Job who he thinks he is anyway. He says that to try to explain the kind of things Job wants explained would be like trying to explain Einstein to a little-neck clam. ... God doesn't reveal his grand design. He reveals himself.[3]

Could it be that our sincerest prayers for God to show us His will would be answered more clearly if we prayed, "Father, show us Your face"? God's answer can be summarized in two words: "Trust Me."

God says the same thing to you and me. If, like Joseph, you see how your hurts have resulted in something profitable, then thank God for His grace. And if you cannot see God's hand through the fog of your pain, then thank God that you can trust Him. He has not forgotten you. He will not forsake you.

In your situation, when did you trust God? with what?

_____

What do you now know about Him that you didn't know prior to your experience of trusting Him through a time of pain?

_____

_____

You may still be struggling with the issue of forgiveness. Someone or something has caused you great pain. You want to forgive and be free from bitterness. You've spent hours reading about why and how to forgive. But if you release that person who has wronged you, you need something to grab hold of to maintain your balance in life.

God is saying to you: "Release your bitterness and grab hold of Me. Allow Me to take responsibility for what has happened to you. Know that I have a plan I'm working out in your life, even if you can't see it now." Christian author Joe Bayly says: "Faith means something when it is exercised in the darkness." [4]

Are you ready, right now, in your own situation to do this? Choose a prayer posture of humbleness and reverence as you:
        … release your bitterness;
        … voice forgiveness for those who've hurt you;
        … embrace your pain, knowing that as you do, you embrace God's plan and watchcare for you.

This past week I received a letter from a prisoner who regularly watches our ministry's television broadcast. Usually I can predict with great accuracy the content of such letters: a request for money or a plea for help in obtaining a release. But this letter was different. The prisoner had something he wanted to give me.

He had noticed in my sermon a passing reference to an upcoming series on forgiveness. "About a month ago," he said, "I wrote a poem on forgiveness and thought you might be able to use it." The following poem was scrawled on the back of the piece of yellow legal paper.

FORGIVE
by David Aultman

God sent His one and only begotten Son,
To forgive us of all the wrong we have done.
He wants us to do the same thing, too.
He wants you to forgive me and for me to forgive you.
Sometimes it's hard to forget all the wrong,
But we must learn to forgive and to move on.
And if we proceed to live in this way,
God will proceed to forgive us each day.
I must give credit where credit is due,
So Matthew 6:14 tells me this much is true:
One thing to remember for as long as you live,
If you want to be forgiven, then you have to forgive.[5]

David Aultman captured in a few lines what it has taken me many pages to say. The reason we're to forgive is simple: Forgiveness is the obligation of the forgiven.

Another prisoner who lived many years ago said it even more succinctly: "Be kind and compassionate to one another, forgiving each other, just as in Christ God forgave you" (Eph. 4:32).

---

[1] Ron Mehl, *The Ten(der) Commandments* (Sisters, OR: Multnomah, 1998), 49-50.

[2] C. S. Lewis, *The Problem of Pain* (New York: Macmillan, 1962), 40, 47.

[3] Robert Jeffress, *When Forgiveness Doesn't Make Sense* (Colorado Springs, CO: Waterbrook Press, 2000), 194.

[4] Ibid, 195.

[5] Ibid, 196.

Leader Guide

Before the group sessions begin, prepare yourself as facilitator by completing these actions:

1. Read the entire book so you will understand the direction the group is going, be able to provide additional help when questions arise, and, in general, be better equipped. You may also want to obtain and read *When Forgiveness Doesn't Make Sense*, the volume from which this study comes, as an enrichment resource. Focus on content; begin identifying the difficult or tender places for you personally; identify the direction Dr. Jeffress is taking you throughout the study.
2. Enlist a prayer partner who isn't participating in the group. Agree on a regular time for each of you to pray for this group and your leadership.
3. Participate in promoting the study and enlisting participants. Plan to conduct an (optional) introductory session and six group sessions. The purpose of the introductory session is to get to know one another, acquaint members with the study, and distribute materials.

Introductory Session

Before the Session

1. Provide markers and materials for making nametags. Or have available ready made nametags.
2. Plan to have workbooks available for distribution or purchase. Some churches furnish workbooks for group members at no charge. Others choose to allow members to pay some or all of the cost of materials. Consider the possibility that members may take the study more seriously if they bear or share in the cost.
3. Prepare an overhead cell of the quote: "Forgiveness is a beautiful word, until you have something to forgive."—C. S. Lewis.
4. Duplicate copies of the Nickie and Chet Case Studies from step 3 of During the Session. Enlist two participants as they arrive to read aloud during the session. Encourage them to look over the stories as other members arrive.
5. On separate pieces of chart paper copy the following Scriptures leaving blanks for some words: Matthew 5:23-24; Matthew 6:14-15; Matthew 18:21-22; Mark 11:25-26;

Ephesians 4:32. Display the charts in the meeting room.
6. Arrange to have an overhead projector and screen in your meeting room, as well as any other supplies such as a chalkboard, marker board, and so forth.
7. Arrange the chairs so that participants can see one another.

During the Session

1. Greet participants as they arrive and direct them to the nametags. Have workbooks available there also.
2. Welcome participants, then call attention to the C. S. Lewis quote that you have displayed on the overhead. Invite responses by reading aloud the quote. Pause and add, "... and then ...." Wait for responses.
3. Call on the two readers for Nickie's and Chet's stories. After both stories have been read aloud, instruct participants to move into groups of three and ask each group to determine if, when forgiveness is required, they are more like Nickie— defeated and depressed, or Chet—angry and defiant. After a few minutes, share responses with the larger group. Affirm the range of emotions and reactions expressed.

Nickie—was abandoned by her father and mother when she was a little girl, but her grandparents in North Carolina happily agreed to take her in. Although money was tight for them, they were generous. Nickie shared: "They gave me anything I wanted. They were cotton-mill people, but if I wanted a Coca-Cola—they cost a nickel—I got it. Comic books were ten cents, and she'd get me two. Saturday morning theater was fifteen cents, and I always got to go."

Growing up, Nickie learned the benefits of forgiveness. "It's something my grandmother taught me," Nickie said. "If you don't forgive others, it will eat you alive."

After her grandfather died in 1964, Nickie began stopping by regularly to care for her grandmother. She cooked, cleaned, and changed her grandmother's clothes and bed sheets. For an eight-year stretch, Nickie visited her grandmother every day without fail—no vacations, no breaks.

One day in late 1994, Nickie arrived at her grandmother's home and discovered that she had fallen. She called the fire department for assistance.

Alarmed at what might happen in case of a fire and distressed over her inability to adequately care for her grandmother in her worsening health, Nickie finally placed her in a nursing home, despite her grandmother's objections.

Then came a staggering blow. After only three weeks in the nursing home, her grandmother died. "If I hadn't taken her over there," Nickie lamented, "she wouldn't have died."

A few days after the funeral, Nickie related to her minister her terrible guilt over her grandmother's death. The pastor prayed for Nickie.

"He prayed; I listened," she says, "but I felt no comfort at all."

Nickie continues to ask God for forgiveness, but still has not received the answer she seeks.

"If you're forgiven, you just know," she says. "You feel it. When you're really, really thirsty, it's the first swallow that tastes so good and sweet. That's what forgiveness tastes like. And since she died, I have never tasted that."[1]

Chet—is a devout Christian who understands what the Bible says about forgiveness. "Christ taught us that it's something we Christians should be willing to do if the offender is asking forgiveness or is repentant for his or her action. Then it becomes our Christian obligation to forgive." But he says he has difficulty agreeing with those who teach that Christians "should offer carte blanche forgiveness for every sin committed against us."

One can sympathize with Chet's feelings. In 1992, his son Kevin, a pizza delivery man, was killed in an armed robbery. His other son, Keith, was murdered in 1994 by a man Chet had fired from his business.

Since the killers have not repented of their actions, Chet feels no obligation to forgive. Would he forgive if the killers ever repented? "I would not necessarily say yes; we'll talk about it when the time comes."

Chet has little patience with Christians who want to talk only about his obligation to forgive. He says they give him the impression "that if we as Christians don't forgive everyone who sins against us, then we are equally guilty somehow, and I don't buy that."

Chet is channeling some of his rage into developing a support network for crime victims. He says this is something that the church should be doing, but the church seems to be more concerned with "the reconciliation between prisoners and their victims. Well, while the church is worried about redeeming the defendants, I'm concerned with the victims that are lying on the sidewalk, bleeding …. Don't come asking for forgiveness for the people that have killed my children."[2]

4. In the same groups of three, ask members to discuss and complete the fill-in-the-blank Scriptures on the charts you prepared earlier. Remind group that this study is biblically based and provides them an opportunity to explore the subject of forgiveness from God's perspective as well as the benefit of practical application.

5. Summarize Dr. Jeffress' three reasons why Christians struggle to forgive. (1) It's difficult to impart that which we have not experienced; (2) We do not understand what forgiveness is and is not; (3) We are busy riding the "blame/guilt" seesaw. Invite discussion and questions about these three reasons.

6. Briefly explain that the book is divided into three parts. Refer participants to the different response activities used throughout the workbook.

   • Encourage group members to study each day in preparation for your weekly meeting. Since each unit of study is 14 to 16 pages of material, they will need to study two or three pages per day.

   • Confirm meeting times and places for the sessions.

   • Assign Part 1: Introduction and Unit 1 for next week.

   • Testify briefly to the impact of your individual study; urge participants to complete each activity/response, and review the study material just prior to each session.

7. Explain that each session will begin with two activities.

   • *New-n-Improved:* What new thought, insight, or truth from the previous session cropped up in your daily lives this past week? (This encourages members to seek and expect changes in behaviors and attitudes from their study and from Scripture. As you explain "New-n-Improved," mention their option to choose and memorize a Scripture from each unit's material.)

• *Bottom-Line-It:* What phrase, sentence, or Scripture in this unit's material did you most need to hear? (Mention that members will want to mark or circle this as they prepare for group sessions and be ready to share it at the beginning of each session. Expect different "bottom lines" because members will filter the study material through their personal needs, memories, resentments, desires for forgiveness, and so forth.)

8. Explain that group sessions are not designed for you to teach each unit's material, but for the group to support one another's struggles and victories with forgiveness.

Prayer Time

1. Close in a directed prayer, incorporating the final quote by Smedes: "The first and often the only person to be healed by forgiveness is the person who does the forgiveness .... When we genuinely forgive, we set a prisoner free and then discover that the prisoner we set free is us."[3]

Session 1:
Being Forgiven, But Not a Forgiver

Before the Session

1. Plan to provide nametags as long as members (including you) are still becoming acquainted.

2. Provide chart paper and markers for groups making presentations.

3. On two three-by-five-inch cards write the questions for "New-n-Improved" and "Bottom-Line-It." Keep these in your Bible to use each week as you begin each session.

4. Ahead of time, write these two incomplete sentences on the chalkboard or chart paper: (1) I understand my guilt well enough to know ... (2) I understand God's grace well enough to know .... Display in meeting room.

5. Ahead of time, write on sentence strips one each of three advantages in step 3 of During the Session.

During the Session

1. Begin the session with "New-n-Improved" and "Bottom-Line-It." Affirm whatever members are willing to share in these exercises and throughout each session.

2. Refer to the exercise on page 8 related to big and small offenses. Ask and discuss: *How did this exercise help you evaluate the*

Bible story about Simon the Pharisee and his attitude, 'Big sinners have a lot more to be thankful for than little sinners like me'? Inquire whether or not anyone is willing to read the letter he or she wrote to Jesus. Remind members that these opening exercises focus on the truth that our attitudes about forgiveness come directly from the sense of needing forgiveness ourselves. Pause to pray for a continued humbling of our spirits.

3 Arrange members into three groups and give each group a sentence strip with one of the following advantages forgiven people possess: (1) Forgiven people understand their own guilt; (2) Forgiven people understand the need for intervention; (3) Forgiven people understand grace. Instruct groups to share personal comments related to their assigned advantage and then to prepare a one-minute presentation/summary to the large group.

4. Reassemble as a large group, then call on each group to make its presentation; affirm creativity and key points and encourage lively discussion.

5. Conclude by referring to the incomplete sentences on the chalkboard or chart paper. Assign the first statement to one-half of the group, assign the second statement to the remaining half. Allow three minutes for persons in each group to share their answers with one another.

6. Assign the Unit Two material. Affirm participants for good participation in this first session.

Prayer Time

1. Instruct participants to remain in two small groups and to review their answers to the statement: "I understand God's grace well enough to know...." Direct them to close, thanking God for His grace before leaving quietly.

Session Two:
The Case Against Forgiveness

Before the Session

1. Collect and plan to display current news articles relating situations in which forgiveness, if offered, would be a very difficult choice (similar to the opening story in Unit 2, p. 19).
2. On four pieces of chart paper, write one each of the following four logical arguments against forgiveness: (1) Forgiveness denies the seriousness of sin; (2) Forgiveness lets people off the hook too easily; (3) Forgiveness places too much responsibility on the victim; (4) Forgiveness is unjust. Display posters around the meeting room.

During the Session

1. Greet members as they arrive. Encourage participants to browse the article display.
2. Begin with the opening activities, "New-n-Improved" and "Bottom-Line-It." Remember to affirm those group members willing to share.
3. Divide participants into two groups: earliest arrivers versus latest arrivers. Choose one of the news articles from the display, recap the story, and identify the opportunities to forgive and/or be forgiven. Then set up a debate between the two groups, one arguing for forgiveness and one against, both using the four reasons displayed around the room. Allow preparation time and encourage use of Scripture on both sides. After adequate time, conduct the debate.
4. If time permits, choose a second newspaper article, but instruct groups to argue the opposite side. Debrief this exercise thoroughly.
5. Conclude by asking for volunteers to share answers to the continuum activity that concludes Unit 2.
6. Assign Unit 3 for the next session. Remind participants to keep in mind "New-n-Improved" and "Bottom-Line-It" while studying.

Prayer Time

1. Close the session with sentence prayers that begin, "Lord, I accept my obligation to forgive because ...."

Session Three:
Saying and Hearing "I'm Sorry"

Before the Session

1. Place one three-by-five-inch card and a pencil in each chair before participants arrive.
2. Ahead of time write on the chalkboard or chart paper the three reasons for demanding repentance before granting forgiveness: (1) Forgiveness Needs to Be Earned; (2) Forgiving an Unrepentant Person Invites Further Abuse; (3) Forgiving an Unrepentant Person Is Unscriptural.
3. Prepare two large placards. On one placard write in large letters "FOR"; on the other write "AGAINST." Display on two opposite walls in the meeting room.
4. Compile a list of Christian counselors to use as referrals if necessary. If you are uncertain about those to include, check with your pastor for input.

During the Session

1. Welcome members to the session. Begin with the opening activities, "New-n-Improved" and "Bottom-Line-It." Allow ample time; encourage each member to share.
2. Instruct members to write on the three-by-five-inch cards a situation in which someone would expect the offender to say, "I'm sorry." (Perhaps they can recount one used in their Unit 3 responses; assure members of anonymity as cards are read during the session.) Collect the cards for use in the following activity.
3. Call attention to the three arguments for demanding repentance before forgiving that you wrote on a chalkboard, and the signs "FOR" and "AGAINST" on opposite walls of the room. Direct members to mill about the center of the room while you read aloud a situation from one of the cards, then ask them to face the appropriate wall in answer to the question: In this situation, are you for or against forgiving this offender who has not asked for repentance? Question several members about the reasons for their answers. Read several situation cards and repeat the process. Encourage members to use the Point/Counterpoint in their workbooks related to the three arguments to explain their answers.
4. Ask participants to be seated; then ask them to share their answers to the Point/Counterpoint exercise at the bottom of page 39 and top of page 40. Comment as needed.

5. Ask and discuss: *What prayer needs do you have based on this discussion?* Record answers on a chalkboard; ask for volunteers to choose one need each and to pray a short prayer for that need.

6. Ask and discuss: *What did you learn from your concordance search this week, suggested on page 42?* Affirm insights members offer. Read aloud the margin quote: *Repentance is our offender's responsibility; forgiveness is our responsibility.* Encourage comments.

7. Refer members to the section, "Unconditional Forgiveness Is Beneficial." Call attention to the paragraph that suggests the option of writing letters to offenders who are unaware or even unmoved by their actions, or separated by distance or death. Proceed with sensitivity; some members may have confronted difficult, even terrifying, memories in this section. Acknowledge that, and gently but firmly suggest that if they wrote such a letter this week, you are available to meet privately with them, or you will pray for them while they discuss it with a trusted friend or counselor. Be prepared with Christian counseling referrals for some who may ask after the session.

8. Say: *It is vital for us to filter through our experience of being forgiven by God our desires for vengeance and justice and for our offenders to repent and make restitution to us. We must remember what incredible victory and blessing we've gained because God abandons vengeance, offers us Christ's sacrifice to dispense God's justice, and knows we cannot make restitution for our sins, choosing to love us.* Read aloud the Swindoll quote on pages 49-50.

9. Conclude by saying: *We considered two barriers to forgiveness in Unit 3, and we will consider two more barriers in Unit 4.* Refer members to the two columns at the end of Unit 3 on page 50. Instruct members to answer silently: *Are you a left- or right-column person?*

10. Arrange members into groups of three and encourage them to share their responses to the above question.

Prayer Time

1. While remaining in the three small groups, encourage group members to share concerns and pray for one another before leaving.

Session Four:
Forgiveness, Forgetfulness, and Reconciliation

Before the Session

1. Prepare a chart using the title to the song, "It Is Well with My Soul." Leave space below the song title to list responses as given later in the session.

During the Session

1. Welcome members. Begin with the opening activities, "New-n-Improved" and "Bottom-Line-It." Remind members they have completed half of the study. Using the hymn title, "It Is Well with My Soul," ask members to repeat the phrase but substitute a word for "well" that best describes their experiences with or understanding of forgiveness. List responses on the chart you prepared earlier. Use responses to lead a prayer of confession.

2. Arrange participants into three groups, assigning each group a case study from the opening pages of Unit 4. Ask groups to discuss their responses to the case studies. After adequate time, ask and discuss: *What will "make or break" forgiveness in these instances? (Confusing forgiveness with reconciliation) Does anyone have a new appreciation for your pastor after reading these situations?*

3. Summarize the two reasons why Christians need to seek reconciliation. Ask and discuss: *Like the judge, have you ever been embarrassed by the behavior of Christians?* Track the discussion to note whether such instances bring out the worst or best in members. Gently remind the group that we imperfect, sinful Christians often make situations worse by responding with harsh judgmentalism.

4. Direct members to return to their original three groups; assign each group one of the steps of reconciliation: repentance, restitution, and rehabilitation. Ask groups to review Unit 4 material related to their assigned step and apply it to the case study they first examined. After adequate work time, call for reports from groups. Honestly assess the practicality of these steps.

5. Remind members that reconciliation is often bogged down with the fourth barrier: forgetting past offenses. Ask for members' reactions to Dr. Jeffress' statement: "Since God has wired our bodies to permanently record our experiences,

there must be positive benefits to remembering our sins." Continue: *Does this extend to remembering others' sins against us as well?*

6. Direct members one last time to reassemble in three groups. Have members apply the four steps to dealing with the memories of other people's offenses to the case studies. Call for reports and affirm the practical applications members offer.

7. Conclude by observing that members have masterfully applied principles regarding forgiveness, forgetting, and reconciliation to fictitious lives. Ask if using them in their own lives prompts a response of, "Yes, but ...." Encourage members at the point of their doubts.

Prayer Time

1. Frame the concerns voiced in the previous step as prayer requests; close in a season of prayer that the desire to forgive will overcome doubt. Assign Unit 5 for the next session.

Session Five:
Receiving the Gift and Giving It Away

Before the Session

1. Pray specifically for each group member. This unit has the potential to be intense as members work through the activities. Pray that members will be honest in their responses throughout the unit.

During the Session

1. Welcome members and begin with "New-n-Improved" and "Bottom-Line-It." Keep in mind that Unit 5 work is potentially difficult. Gently explore with members how willingly they completed the exercises in asking for and granting forgiveness.

2. Say: *Unit 5 described men who were on the opposite ends of the forgiveness continuum—David and life-wrenching guilt on the one end, Joseph and vengeful redress on the other.* Ask and discuss: *What were the spiritual and relational victories achieved by both men?* Ask for members' insights in their own lives regarding guilt and vengeance. If members are hesitant to respond, share from your own experience.

3. Remind members of two exercises in Unit 5: writing a confession and asking for forgiveness on page (page 78), and

forgiving an offense against you on pages 80-83. Ask members to form groups of three and to recount their work and the impact of one of those exercises. Move among the groups and be alert to anyone needing encouragement.

4. Reassemble and debrief members' thoughts and feelings while "confessing" real experiences to one another. Confirm the faith required to complete these exercises and the most important outcome: remaining focused on God's forgiving work in our lives. Assign Unit 6.

Prayer Time

1. Invite members to pray sentence prayers expressing their gratitude for God's grace that covers our guilt and His forgiveness for our sins.

Session Six:
Does God Need Our Forgiveness?

Before the Session

1. Prepare four sheets of newsprint to resemble four CUSTOMER Service Windows with one category each at the top of the sheet: "Others," "Ourselves," "Circumstances," "Satan." Leave space beneath titles for recording responses. Display in a row on the focal wall of the meeting room.

2. On a small table in front of the Customer Service Windows, light a single candle.

3. Prepare a long vertical strip of paper for each member you expect to be present. On each one write the following words, one after the other in this order: "Who?" "What?" "When?" "Where?" "How?" "Why?" "God." Leave space for tearing between each word.

4. On eight three-by-five-inch cards write one each of the following Scriptures: (1) Psalm 119:68; (2) Hebrews 4:15; (3) Exodus 15:13; (4) Psalm 139:16; (5) Proverbs 20:24; (6) Jeremiah 29:11; (7) Romans 8:28-29; and (8) Philippians 3:10. Plan to distribute at the appropriate time during the session.

During the Session

1. Greet members. Thank them for their faithful participation during this study. Lead them in sharing "New-n-Improved" and "Bottom-Line-It" responses.

2. Say: *Dr. Jeffress concludes this study by saying we can hold God accountable for what happens in our lives, and that God's plan for us includes suffering. For the remainder of our time, we'll simulate suffering by using only candlelight and by standing—very gentle reminders that life can be hard, but that the Light of the world remains present to illumine our way.*

3. With the candle lit in front of the Customer Service Windows, move the group from window to window, asking: *When you blame (insert word from each window, such as "others") for your hurts or suffering, how do you feel? How do you act?* Record answers on the newsprint. Note how often the feelings and actions are negative, self-punishing, nonredemptive—regardless of how justified the blame might be.

4. Distribute the vertical paper strips prepared earlier. As members stand in a circle, ask them to recall the most difficult situation in which they've struggled to forgive. Slowly read the words (except the last one–*God*), asking members to recall the answers to those questions related to their particular situations. Then say: *God is asking you to relinquish your hatred toward someone; symbolize your willingness to do so by tearing the word "who" off your paper and dropping it to the floor. God is asking you to forgive what happened; tear the word "what" off and drop it to the floor. To change your focus from the time and place where this happened, tear the "when" and "where" words off and drop them to the floor. To let Him heal you of how you were hurt, tear the word "how" away and drop it to the floor. Most difficult of all, abandoning your need to know why this happened, tear off the word, "why" also, and drop it to the floor. Now look at what remains in your hands. When you forgive the details of your suffering, you are with—God. Can you affirm that His presence, grace, forgiveness, and astounding love are all that you need?*

5. Quietly distribute the three-by-five-inch cards with the Scriptures you prepared earlier. Allow time for locating passages, then ask those with cards to read them in order. Ask: *What response do you want to make to God right now?* Allow extended time for them to meditate privately. Ask if any members want to share their responses with the group.

6. In closing, invite members to offer any thoughts of appreciation to fellow group members or leaders for the study.

Prayer Time

1. Ask participants to kneel in the candlelit room, then lead members in praying the Lord's Prayer. Quietly dismiss.

---

[1] Les Alexander, "Nickie Boyd says she believes in forgiveness utterly and completely, but she can't forgive herself," posted 4 April 1996 by the *News & Record* and *Triad Online*.

[2] Les Alexander, "Chet Hodgin of Jamestown is adamant about not forgiving the men who killed his two sons," posted 4 April 1996 by the *News & Record* and *Triad Online*.

[3] Lewis Smedes, *The Art of Forgiving* (New York: Ballantine, 1996), 178.

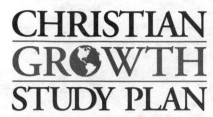

CHRISTIAN GROWTH STUDY PLAN

Preparing Christians to Serve

In the **Christian Growth Study Plan (formerly Church Study Course),** this book *Free to Forgive* is a resource for course credit in the subject area Personal Life of the Christian Growth category of diploma plans. To receive credit, read the book, complete the learning activities, show your work to your pastor, a staff member or church leader, then complete the following information. This page may be duplicated. Send the completed page to:

Christian Growth Study Plan
127 Ninth Avenue, North, MSN 117
Nashville, TN 37234-0117
FAX: (615)251-5067

For information about the Christian Growth Study Plan, refer to the current Christian Growth Study Plan Catalog. Your church office may have a copy. If not, request a free copy from the Christian Growth Study Plan office (615/251-2525).

Free to Forgive
COURSE NUMBER: CG-0580

PARTICIPANT INFORMATION

Social Security Number (USA ONLY)	Personal CGSP Number*	Date of Birth (MONTH, DAY, YEAR)

Name (First, Middle, Last)	Home Phone

Address (Street, Route, or P.O. Box)	City, State, or Province	Zip/Postal Code

CHURCH INFORMATION

Church Name

Address (Street, Route, or P.O. Box)	City, State, or Province	Zip/Postal Code

CHANGE REQUEST ONLY

☐ Former Name

☐ Former Address	City, State, or Province	Zip/Postal Code

☐ Former Church	City, State, or Province	Zip/Postal Code

Signature of Pastor, Conference Leader, or Other Church Leader	Date

*New participants are requested but not required to give SS# and date of birth. Existing participants, please give CGSP# when using SS# for the first time. Thereafter, only one ID# is required. **Mail to:** Christian Growth Study Plan, 127 Ninth Ave., North, Nashville, TN 37234-0117. Fax: (615)251-5067

Rev. 6-99